Finding Life

a journey through 1 John...

PETER JOHN SCHROCK

Godly Christian MINISTRIES

Published by: Godly Christian Ministries
www.GodlyChristianMinistries.com

Print Edition: 1.0
ISBN: 0-9842733-0-1
ISBN-13: 978-0-9842733-0-0

Printed in the United States of America
December 2009

Many people significantly helped
me to make this book a reality.
Thank you!

Preface

Writing a devotional on first John, was the farthest thing from my mind when I started to memorize its first chapter. My goal was simply to hide these words deep within my heart and to inspire others to do it with me. Though not many people were interested in memorizing the book, several people were greatly encouraged by some thoughts that I wrote down as I was going through the first chapter. As a result, the idea to write a devotional as I memorized each chapter developed into this book you are now reading.

The task of writing this book was broken up into five parts. Each part corresponded to one chapter in 1 John. When I started on each chapter, I first translated the chapter from the original language into English and then I memorized my personal translation. Once I had finished memorizing the translation, I began the slow process of converting my meditations into daily readings. This process often involved days or weeks of praying, comparing passages, and seeking help from others just to produce a single day's devotional. Eventually, I finished writing on each part and passed along each section to others for proofreading and review. Several wonderful people, spent many hours going through each page combing out my mistakes and offering help to communicate these vital truths. Once the entire work on 1 John was completed, the book was made public for others to be built up into the image of Christ.

As you read this daily study of 1 John, I encourage you to be aware of two specific themes. John expresses the first theme when he uses words like light, fellowship, abiding, love, and life. Though at first glance it may appear that these words are unrelated, John is actually expressing a single reality. The summation of this reality can be described as personally knowing God. The second theme is trusting God. John is describing trusting God when he writes about obedience, victory, and love for others. These two themes are the essence of Christianity. All too often, believers break off on side tangents and fall away from the heart of God. The goal of this book is to help you find stability in your Christian life by teaching you how to daily walk in the reality of these two themes. Therefore, do not rush through this book, but take the needed time to meditate and ponder the things it expresses. As you walk in the two themes of 1 John you will find deeper fellowship with God and learn to become His disciple.

Day 1

That which was from the beginning, which we have heard, which we have seen with our eyes, which we have looked at and our hands have touched – concerning the word of life. The life appeared and we have seen it and testify to it and we proclaim to you the eternal life which was with the Father and has appeared to us. (1 John 1:1-2)

Many people think of the doctrines of the apostles as some lofty abstract theological system that only seminarians can grasp after they finish their doctorate in divinity. However, John's doctrine or teaching is a down to earth reality that anyone can experience. In fact, the way John obtained his understanding was through his own personal interaction with God. John experienced spiritual life and from his own reality, expressed what he had come to know. The letter of 1 John is a practical book to help us discern what spiritual life is and to know if we are experiencing it.

In these beginning verses, John explains this life as being tangible and not some intellectual exercise. He was able to hear, see, and touch life as it was personified in the man Christ Jesus. John expounds on this a little further in his gospel when he writes, *"In the beginning was the Word, and the Word was with God, and the Word was God. He was with God in the beginning. All things were made through Him, and apart from Him nothing was made that had been made. In Him was life, and the life was the light of men. The light shines in the darkness, and the darkness has not held it back... And the Word became flesh and dwelt among us, and we have seen His glory, glory as of the only begotten Son from the Father, full of grace and truth"* (John 1:1-5, 14). John experienced life itself when he saw true spiritual vitality illuminated in Jesus.

Imitations of spiritual life abound in the world around us, but John came to know the difference between the real thing and the counterfeit by his own experience with Jesus. In this way, when John writes about life in Jesus, he is not repeating something that he heard in a sermon. Nor was he expressing a systematic teaching that he had gotten from a textbook. He was simply testifying what he had seen and heard. Though sermons and textbooks can be good at times, one cannot equate life with the contents of their words, for words are merely descriptions that give us understanding about something that is real (John 5:39-40). John describes the reality that he came to know in Jesus, but his words point to something concrete that he experienced. The words that John wrote are a priceless tutor to teach us what life in Jesus is and how to experience it.

Are the words you speak an expression of what you have seen and heard? All too often, people hear a sermon or read something in a book and they think they found true life. Nevertheless, when they seek to put their new understanding into practice, they find that their life was only another imitation. The world is cluttered with instructions from people who have not seen and heard the end result of their teaching. They arrogantly claim to have found some unique things to do for Jesus that will produce life among assembled believers. However, the end of their teaching is division and confusion because they have not yet heard, seen, and touched the real Jesus. John saw how Jesus lived and learned to experience the same life that Jesus had. If you want to keep yourself from running down all the rabbit trails of this world, learn what John has testified to and put it into practice.

Questions to Ponder...

1. What are two things I have experienced concerning following Jesus that are written in the Bible?

2. What are two things I have not experienced concerning following Jesus that are written about in the Bible?

3. Is there anything in my life that I need to experience before I should try to explain it to others?

That which we have seen and heard we proclaim to you too, so that you also may have fellowship with us. And our fellowship is with the Father and with His son, Jesus Christ. We write this to make our joy complete. (1 John 1:3-4)

Fellowship is a greatly confused word among many Christian circles. Most times it is reduced to a bunch of people hanging out and doing activities together. Though there is an element of truth in this perspective, it does not necessarily mean that people are speaking of the same kind of fellowship that John had in mind. The kind of fellowship that John spoke of was when people walked together in communion with God.

The Greek word for fellowship comes from the idea of sharing something in common. At times, this sharing can refer to a financial burden (2 Corinthians 9:13, Romans 15:26). In other cases, it may refer to the sharing of a common work (Philippians 1:4-5, Philemon 1:17). Nevertheless, the word most often refers to communion and a sharing of experience. Paul demonstrates this usage when he writes, *"God, who has called you into fellowship with His Son Jesus Christ our Lord, is faithful"* (1 Corinthians 1:9). And elsewhere he writes, *"May the grace of the Lord Jesus Christ, and the love of God, and the fellowship of the Holy Spirit be with you all"* (2 Corinthians 13:14). It is this usage that John adheres to when he writes, *"And our fellowship is with the Father and with His son, Jesus Christ"* (1 John 1:3). John is saying that he has communion and shares his experience of life with the Father and His son, Jesus Christ.

When many Christians think of fellowship they often associate it with building friendships and sharing experiences with other believers. They think that going to a football game together or watching a movie with others is Christian fellowship. Nevertheless, in most cases it really isn't Christian fellowship at all. Rather, it is fellowship with football or a movie. The fellowship that John described was with God. John was already experiencing fellowship with God, but he desired that other people would enter into the fellowship he was already having. Therefore he writes, *"That which we have seen and heard we proclaim to you too, so that you also may have fellowship with us"* (1 John 1:3). The key word here is also. John already walked sharing the experience of communion with God with other people, but he desired that those he wrote to would also come to know this fellowship.

What kind of fellowship do you have with other Christians? We rally around all sorts of different practices and topics. Some of us have fellowship in specific forms of dress, others in a particular doctrinal knowledge, and still others in fun activities. All these kinds of fellowship are frequently dead works that often distract us from drawing near to God. Though it is not wrong for us to have fellowship in many different ways, our primary fellowship must be rooted in experientially knowing God. If knowing God is not at the center of your fellowship with other Christians, you need to repent. Change your mind and perspective about how and why you spend time with other believers. When we walk together in proper fellowship with God, all of our joy will be truly made complete (1 John 1:4).

Question to Ponder...

Do I fellowship with 'Christians' on the basis that they are walking with God or do I have something else in common with them?

Day 3

This is the message we have heard from Him and pro-claim to you: God is light; there is no darkness in Him at all! If we say we have fellowship with Him yet walk in the darkness, we lie and are not doing the truth.
(1 John 1:5-6)

One of the most pivotal statements in all of John's writings is made in verse five of this passage. Here we read the message that John had received from God for us. This message was that God is light and there is absolutely no darkness in Him at all. God's purity far exceeds our imagination and in Him light is present in such abundance that darkness completely ceases to exist. If we begin to walk in communion with God, having fellowship with Him, darkness will no longer be part of our lives.

Light and darkness are every-day things that we experience. When we see light, darkness ceases to exist by the mere virtue that darkness is the absence of light. Paul alludes to this reality when he asks, *"...what fellowship does light have with darkness?"* (2 Corinthian 6:14). The obvious answer to his question is: NONE. Light and darkness are complete opposites and are directly related to sight and blindness. At times we may look for things in the dark, but our eyes are completely useless. No matter how hard we try to examine our surroundings, our attempts fail. We can stare at something as long as we want, but in the absence of light, we will never be able to distinguish what we are trying to focus on. Until light shines, we are hopelessly blind.

John's description of God being light is a key to grasping the whole of this book. In chapter two, John draws a connection between Love and Light. Also, later in chapter four, John ties it all back together again when he says that God is Love. The very nature of God (love) illuminates our hearts and nothing remains hidden in His presence. The Greek phrasing is quite emphatic when stating that there is no darkness in God, for it adds an additional negative. A literal rendering is something like: *"God is light and no darkness is in Him, None!"* Such an additional emphasis must certainly be necessary for us, because the heart is desperately wicked. We should never be deceived thinking that God will allow darkness to conceal sin in our hearts when we walk with him. Everything is illuminated in His presence and if we retreat from His light then we reject God, for God is light. Therefore no one who is born of God can go on sinning (1 John 3:9).

If you are cherishing sin in your heart and are able pray and read the Bible without repenting (i.e. turning from sin), then God is far from you. God is light and when light shines on sin it brings such conviction that one must either turn from that sin or retreat into darkness. As the message has been declared that there is no darkness in and around God, how can those who walk in darkness have nearness and fellowship with God? Do not be deceived, God is not mocked. If it is okay for you to disobey God in even the little things, you will find that He is not near you. For there is NO darkness in God, NONE!

Questions to Ponder...

1. Am I trying to hide sin in my life?

2. Do I want to be transformed and therefore love to have my motives and thoughts exposed by the light of God?

$\mathcal{D}ay$ 4

*But if we are walking in the light, as He is in the light,
we have fellowship with one another, and the blood of
Jesus, His Son, is cleansing us from all sin. (1 John 1:7)*

Where does true Christian fellowship originate? Is it based
on location and daily friendship? Is it founded on a set of shared
doctrines? Could it simply be the sharing of a common minis-
try? What is it that unites believers and brings them to commune
with each other? It is Light. This is what saints have in common; as we already read: God is light.

Where Light is, truth is illuminated into our inner beings.
When Christ was on the earth He walked with the Father this
way: Perfect light shining on every aspect of His being and character. He was so illuminated that He knew the way of escape
from every temptation. Now in the presence of God, He dwells
in the glorious light of the Father, and just as He is in this Light,
so we are called to walk in this Light (1 John 4:17). When people
who profess Christ walk in disunity and not true fellowship, they
do so because they don't abide in the light of the Father. If they
did, they would have nothing to argue about because their hearts
would be exposed and they would see their own faults that are
causing them to sin. All disunity has its origin in the lack of true
fellowship with the Father.

We are not able to enter and experience this true fellowship
with God by merely saying we're sorry if we sin. Rather, forgiveness and cleansing are conditionally based upon where we
are walking. If we are walking in darkness, then we can easily
deceive ourselves into thinking that we are forgiven when we are
not. For 1 John 2:11 explains that darkness blinds us from seeing

where we are going. The deception of darkness is not that we are unconscious of our faults, but rather that we are incapable of seeing them accurately. One standing in the dark could determine that their body is wet, but being unable to see, still would not be able to truly describe their appearance. For all they know, they could just be wet looking, but perhaps they are soaked with an odorless, red die. While remaining in the dark, such a person may feel confident that they know what they look like, but in reality, only the light will expose their true condition. Such is the same for those not walking in fellowship with God. They often think they perceive their own faults clearly, but in reality they are blind and have no idea of their true state.

Only as we walk in the light does real cleansing occur. Many people, who think they are in the light, have believed a lie that the blood of Christ hides the rebellion and sin that they continue to walk in. However, this is what darkness does: it covers sins that are allowed to persist so that they are not seen while they remain present. Nevertheless, light exposes everything so that true cleansing can occur.

As the light exposes each new thing in our heart, we must eradicate it out of our lives. Power to remove sin is found in trusting God, for faith (trust) is the victory that overcomes the world (1 John 5:4). The source of this trust and confidence in God originates from being in His presence. For, in as much that God is Light, He is also Love and in His presence, consciousness of this love is known. When we come to know and trust in this love, we come to abide in Him (1 John 4:16). As we remain in Him, we bear the fruit of His Spirit and we are transformed and renewed into His likeness (John 15:5). Then, in Christ, the stain of guilt is purged through the outpouring of His blood and we stand truly clean.

The process of being purged and cleansed comes as a natural result of walking in the light; however, we must strive to enter and remain in this light. All too often, the salvation experience is depicted as a single event accomplished in the *"Sinner's Prayer"*. Nevertheless, the usage of the word for purging or cleansing that appears in 1 John 1:7 brings forth a different perspective. A literal rendering of this verse would be something like, *"But if we walk in the light as He is in the light, we have fellowship with one another and the blood of Jesus is cleansing us from all sin."* The experience of walking in the light is one of constant exposure and when things get dredged up in our hearts, there must be a continual cleansing.

Are your heart and actions continually being exposed before you? When sin becomes illuminated, is it truly being removed from your life? Don't be deceived by the darkness and allow yourself to think you are cleansed when you are simply hiding and concealing sin under shadows. A clear conscience and not a seared conscience is only possessed by those who have fled from darkness to abide in the revealing light of the Father. Here alone does division cease and pure Christian fellowship begin. If you are walking in sin and are not truly being cleansed, then come to the light in order that you may see yourself clearly and find the power that purges every sin.

Questions to Ponder...

1. Are my Christian relationships characterized by division or unity? ...why?

2. Is God's presence constantly exposing my heart? If not, am I in the light?

3. What is the condition stated in this passage to have the blood of Jesus continually purify me of sin?

Day 5

If at any point in time we might say that we don't currently have sin, we are deceiving ourselves and the truth is not in us. If perhaps we are confessing our sins, He is faithful and just and will forgive us our sins and purify us from all unrighteousness. If at any point, we should say that we have never sinned, we make Him out to be a liar and His word is not in us. (1 John 1:8-10)

All too often, people use these passages to excuse their defeated life of sin. However, such people have totally missed what John was getting at. This is due in part because many English translations have favored good English grammar over trying to explain all that the Greek packs into these verses. When people understand what John was trying to communicate, they can no longer use these passages to justify rebellion in their life. Instead, they are either faced with the depths of their depravity and repent or harden their hearts and turn away from God unto darkness.

Many have taken 1 John 1:8 as justification for the depravity in their lives, thinking that it communicates that we should admit we are always sinning. Nevertheless, it actually does not speak of sin as something one does, but rather something one has. When John speaks of someone *"having sin"*, he is referring to the inward corruption deeply buried within a person's being. Therefore, everyone must admit that they are in need of the continuing work of the Holy Spirit to cleanse and transform them. In this manner, no one in this life time can think that they have arrived and no longer have need to strive to enter the narrow gate. Nevertheless, just because this inward corruption is present doesn't mean that it dominates and controls. As Paul teaches in Romans 6:12-14... *"Therefore do not let sin reign in your mortal bodies...For sin shall not be your master, for you are not under law, but under grace."* Having inward corruption simply means that all strength and power to overcome sin has its origin in God and not ourselves. Without the light of His presence to guide, correct, and empower us, we are hopelessly lost and dominated by our own corruption.

John goes on in verse nine to explain how cleansing from the fruit of our corruption can occur when we are confessing our sins. The English word for confess, does not carry the full weight of the Greek word. The Greek word for confess is a compound word composed of *"to speak"* and *"same"* (to speak the same thing). Hence, the word bares the weight of agreement to a charge brought before someone. This kind of confession is not merely an admitting that sin has occurred, but rather an agreement to what has been revealed about the sin that has occurred. Since what has been revealed about our sin is not simply its existence, this greatly affects the meaning of this passage. The Light does not only reveal sin, but it also reveals the way to overcome it. When we confess our sin, we are saying what God says about our sin. And what God says is that He is ready to forgive AND purge all unrighteousness from us. He says that in Himself there is no sin and that no one who remains in Him keeps on sinning (1 John 3:6). Are you truly confessing your sin or are you only acknowledging it?

In addition to confession of sin, John also warns us to be honest about our life in the past. For he writes in verse ten that we make God a liar by saying that we have not sinned. Unlike verse eight, John is not writing about a current possession of the corruption of sin, but rather, that the inward corruption has had a past dominion in our lives. Therefore, John is communicating that if we say that we have always been righteous, we are calling

God a liar and the things He has said are not cherished in our hearts.

Do you cherish God's word in your heart? If you do, then you will realize that at one time you were an enemy of God, dominated by the corruption of sin, and that God made a way for you to be free from this dominion. He provided this way, in that when you agree with God about your sin, He will forgive your sin and cleanse you. God will place His Holy Spirit in your heart to train you how to walk with Him, so that though the corruption of sin exists in you, you no longer are controlled by it. *"Dear children, do not let anyone deceive you. He who is doing what is right is righteous, just as he is righteous. He who is doing what is sinful is of the devil, because the devil has been sinning from the beginning..."* (1 John 3:7-8). Examine your heart today in light of all these verses being careful not to deceive yourself and call God a liar in an attempt justify your own sin.

Questions to Ponder...

1. Do I realize that there is corruption deep within myself?

2. How do I deal with sin in my life? Do I trust that God is faithful to do what He says?

3. Is there sin in my life that I need to confess that God can both forgive and grant me victory over? If so, what is it?

Day 6

My dear children, I am writing these things to you so that you might not sin. But if anybody does perhaps sin, we have an advocate with the Father, Jesus Christ, the Righteous One. He is the atoning sacrifice for our sins, and not only for ours but also for the sins of the whole world. (1 John 2:1-2)

One of John's intents in writing 1 John is that people might stop sinning. He is not trying to give people any comfort or assurance that they are just fine if they don't repent and experience transformation. Nevertheless, as some people read the beginning of this chapter they comfort themselves that they have an Advocate (Helper, Legal Assistant) with the Father, but they don't turn away from their sin. Such people dwell in great deception because Jesus is not yet their advocate. Others take things even further when they read in verse 2 that Jesus is the atoning sacrifice or appeasement for the sins of the whole world. Such people claim that John is saying that everyone is unconditionally forgiven and will all go to heaven in the end (which is known as Universalism). Unfortunately, this deception has carried many people down to eternal damnation. But let us take heed to John's intent in writing (that we might not sin).

Sin and corruption are deeply rooted in the fabric of our natural humanity, but they can be purged from us. This cleansing does not fully occur in an instant, but as we become united to Jesus through the Holy Spirit this transformation takes place. When we walk in the Light, there are times when sin may be revealed in our hearts. This is a wonderful opportunity to acknowledge what the light has revealed is true and to walk in the power that we see in the light to overcome the corruption. It is to this one that Jesus is an advocate: to those who are walking in the light and not only admit that corruption is in them, but those who on account of the light can see the way of escape from continuing in that corruption. If we refuse to deal with sin in our lives we are no longer abiding in the light. Therefore, we must walk in the light, and from this place, the blood of Jesus is present to make atonement for our sins.

No other atonement exists for the world other than Jesus. It is for this reason that John says that Jesus is the atonement or propitiation for the sins of the whole world. John is not advocating universalism; rather, he is doing just the opposite. People cannot live however they choose and still be forgiven. Instead, they must walk in the light and abide in relationship with the Father. For no one can be reconciled to God through any other atonement than what was provided in Jesus. Jesus is the way, the truth, and the life for everyone. He is the only propitiation provided for the whole world.

Are you aware of sin in your life? If you are, God has shined His light upon you; but, have you seen the way to gain victory over this sin? When Jesus came to the earth, He was the light of the world. He brought revelation and exposed those who walked in darkness. Some of those who received revelation of their state ran to the light, but others fled to greater darkness. What have you done when the light has shone? If you can't see the power of God which brings transformation, you are still in darkness.

Question to Ponder...

Is Jesus my advocate? How do I know?

In this we know that we have come to know Him, if we are keeping His commands. The one who says, "I know Him," but is not keeping His commands is a liar, and the truth is not in him. (1 John 2:3-4)

In this world, people say all kinds of things about their identity and what their relationship with God is like. Each of these people see things from different perspectives and from various levels of understanding. Particularly in America, many think that each person's vantage point has merit and that truth is some relative belief derived from an individual's circumstances. Nevertheless, John opposes such thoughts by revealing the truth when he declares the proper way to discern where we are at with God. This truth is that our relationship with God has a consistent effect on our lives. John eludes to this effect when he says, *"...we know that we have come to know Him, if we are keeping His commands"* (1 John 2:3).

When John penned verse 3, he chose a specific word for *"know"*. In Greek, there are several different words to describe knowing something, but the word John chose describes an experiential knowledge. This gives us insight into understanding how knowing God effects the way we live.

Experiences drive the way we live every day. When we experience something we enjoy, it motivates us to experience it again. When we experience something that is painful, it inspires us to avoid it. In the presence of God, consciousness of love and power exists. Those who abide in this consciousness are inspired to trust and obey the words of Jesus.

Nevertheless, many people think that they know God even though they don't obey His words. Such people don't understand the principle laid out in scripture that a tree is known by its fruit. What we are experiencing in our hearts will show itself through how we live. When we are conscious of how much God loves us and his power to deliver us, it inspires us to have faith that overcomes the world (1 John 5:4). Faith or trust in God overcomes everything the world has to offer: fear, anger, idolatry, sexual immorality, impurity, greed, and much more. However, if someone is not trusting and yielding to God's guidance when seeking to walk with Him, they will not have fellowship with God. Therefore the man who says I know Him, but does not do what He commands is a liar, and the truth is not in him.

Ultimately, the question boils down to who is in God's presence experiencing fellowship with Him? The answer is not some relativistic perspective, but a concrete demonstration of reality. Those who are in the presence of God experience power to overcome sin, but those who reject what God has commanded have turned their back on Him. Have you fallen into deception thinking that you are experientially knowing God, but don't experience power to keep His commands? Wake up and approach the throne of Grace, so that you might find help in your time of need!

Questions to Ponder...

1. How do I know if I know God? Does this match with what John says?

2. Do I know God?

Day 8

But if anyone obeys His word, God's love has truly been matured in him. This is how we know we are in Him: Whoever claims to abide in Him ought to walk just as Jesus walked. (1 John 2:5-6)

God's Love has a transforming effect on our lives. Much in the same way that we desire to please those who love us, when we come to know God's love we desire to please Him. This is not some burdensome task, but a joy and a delight. John describes people who have thoroughly been affected by the love of God as those who keep His word. When you think about obeying the commands of God, do you think about how big of a smile it will put on God's face or do you ponder the inconvenience it is to your agenda? If your mind is still fixed upon your own desires you have not been thoroughly affected by the love of God.

How do we experience this love that transforms us? The answer to this question is found IN Jesus. Jesus is the WAY, the truth, and the life. Apart from abiding in Christ we cannot experience the Father's love. Therefore, it is through becoming united with Jesus that we are granted access into the favor of God. This is why John says that anyone who claims to abide in God, ought to walk the same way Jesus walked, because we need to become one with Jesus in our thoughts, words, and actions. Jesus was the perfect demonstration of this oneness and unity in how He related to the Father. This can be seen in passages throughout the Gospel of John: *"The Son can do nothing of Himself, except what He sees His Father doing...I do nothing from myself, but I speak just as the Father has taught me...my speaking does not originate with myself, rather it is the Father dwelling in Me doing His work"* (John 5:19, 8:28, 14:10). In the same way, Jesus calls us to walk in this same manner in John 15:5, *"I am the vine, you are the branches. The one remaining in me and I in him, he will bear much fruit. Apart from me you can do nothing."* Just like Christ could do nothing apart from the Father, neither can we do anything apart from Christ. Nevertheless, if we remain or abide in Jesus, we have access to the Father by which we can experience His love. It is this love that is the nourishing sap by which good fruit grows. No one should think they can abide in God, without seeking to walk as Jesus walked.

Do you walk like Jesus walked? Perhaps a better question would be, do you think you can do anything useful in the kingdom of God independent of Jesus? Jesus walked in complete dependence upon the Father and therefore became united with the Father in His actions, judgments, and thoughts. Don't think that you have any hope of knowing and abiding in God without it resulting in your total dependence upon Him.

Questions to Ponder...

1. *Is there some area in my life that I am not living totally dependent upon God?*

2. *How much time do I need to spend reading the Gospels in the next month to see how Jesus really walked?*

3. *In light of how Jesus followed the Father, how do I need to change in order to walk just like Jesus?*

$$\mathcal{D}ay\ 9$$

*Dear loved ones, I am not writing you a new com-
mand, but an old command, which you have had
from the beginning. This old command is the word
that you have heard. Again, I am writing you a new
command; its truth is in Him and you, because the
darkness is passing away and the true light is already
shining. Anyone who claims to be in the light, and
is hating his brother is still in the darkness. Whoever
loves his brother abides in the light, and there is no
stumbling block within him. But whoever is hating his brother is in the darkness and walks around
in the darkness; he does not perceive where he is
going, because the darkness has blinded his eyes.
(1 John 2:7-11)*

John wrote to us an old and a new command. Nevertheless,
both can be expressed in the same words. These commands are
that we should love one another. Though the words of these
commands may be identical, their meanings are slightly different.

The old command is what was expressed from the very
beginning, for in 1 John 3:11-12 we are told to love one another
unlike Cain who in the beginning killed his brother. In the beginning, the command to love was rather simple, but now with the
coming of Christ we have a full picture of what love is. Jesus
says, *"a new command I give to you, that you should love one another.
Just as I have loved you, so you also should love one another"* (John
13:34). But how did Jesus love us? He received love from the

Father and with that same love, He Loved us (John 15:9). This is why John says that the truth of this new command is in Him and in us, because Christ is already shining, driving out our darkness through giving us access to the Father's love (John 17:26). When we experience this love, it produces love in our hearts for others.

Nevertheless, if we don't have love in our hearts for others, we are not in fellowship with God, for God is love. We are simply deceiving ourselves if we think we are near to God and yet hate God's people. John tells us that we are actually in the darkness, blinded, and unable to recognize our own state. Such is the dilemma of those who harbor bitterness toward others. They are so stuck on the faults of others that they can't see their own wickedness.

Do you obey God's command to love? There are two ways you can attempt this obedience. First, you can simply try to avoid sinning against others; or second, you can walk in fellowship with God and have love overflow from your heart toward others. If you simply attempt to love in the first manner, you may end up like Cain, but if you come to love by the power of the Spirit, you will end up like Christ. You will lay down your life for others and be full of joy enduring your cross, knowing your heavenly Father is smiling down upon you, giving you peace.

Questions to Ponder...

1. Do I have bitterness in my heart so that I despise someone?

2. When I examine how I love others based upon what John wrote in this passage, am I in the light or in the darkness?

Day 10

I am writing to you, dear children, because your sins have been forgiven on account of His name. I am writing to you, fathers, because you have known Him who is from the beginning. I am writing to you, young men, because you have overcome the evil one. I have written to you, little children, because you have known the Father. I have written to you, fathers, because you have known Him who is from the beginning. I have written to you, young men, because you are strong, and the word of God abides in you, and you have overcome the evil one. (1 John 2:12-14)

When the devil attempts to bring confusion to our walk with God let us correct our thinking through these words that John writes. Each person is at a different place in life and depending on where they are, they need to be reminded of certain truths. Though these passages are addressing age levels, we need not see them as merely speaking to literal ages, but also to levels of maturity. For throughout his letter, John uses the word children to address the whole of its recipients. History tells us that John wrote this letter later in life and the style of writing communicates that John viewed himself as a mature believer addressing those who are younger in the faith. Therefore consider his words and do not forget why you have hope.

To those who are children, John writes reminding them that they have been forgiven and that they know the Father. Those who are young need to know that they have a right standing with God and that they are able to relate to Him personally. He is neither some distant being whom they can only read about, nor one whom they can't approach because of sin. Rather, He has granted forgiveness and reconciliation even to those who have not lived long enough to be esteemed in the world's eyes. People don't need to get old before they begin to walk with God. He desires that they all know Him no matter how young. If you are young don't let anyone make you think that you can't know God yet, for John says, *"I have written to you, little children, because you have known the Father!"* Seek after Him and you will find Him when you search for Him with all your heart.

To those who are young men John writes to address their strength, agreement with the word of God and, ability to overcome the devil. Youth is a time when the body is strong; when stamina and endurance can be at their highest. It is at this time when people have a great opportunity to damage the Devil's kingdom on the earth. Yet all too often, youth invest their time participating in every activity under the sun, seeking fun and pleasure. To their shame they spend much of their prime years building toward vanity, which later in life, when they repent will have to tear down. If you are young, set your focus in life to invest your time toward the kingdom of God. You don't need to be old and gray before the word of God is dwelling in you richly. One who has merely thrown off everything that hinders for a few years can know God very well. If you start seeking when you are young, in a short time, you will still be young and know God. Read the scriptures, spend time in prayer, and throw off vain pursuits. You can be strong and overcome the evil one in your youth.

To the fathers, John gives them a simple reminder that they know Him who is from the beginning. When people get old they often separate themselves from the youth and feel like they can't relate to the generations that come after them. Nevertheless, it is often at this time that older people possess what those who are younger need to hear the most. People who are young need to learn the traps and pit falls that are out in the world which will keep them from knowing God. Often times, as the years go by, we have all fallen prey to something that has ensnared us. Perhaps it was something like religiosity or perhaps a form of sexual immorality. So many things can draw us away from knowing and walking with God. Have you come to the sweet place of walking in fellowship with God for many years? Examine the fruit of your life. Does the fruit of the Spirit flow from you like streams of living water? If so, those who are younger need your help to come unto maturity. If the fruit of the Spirit (Gal. 5:22-23) is not consistently evident in your life, you don't have close fellowship with God. Get right with God, start walking in consistent fellowship with Him, and you will become useful to those who are younger.

No matter where you are in life, God has made a place for you and for others as well. Seek out others and utilize those who are different than you. It is only as each part does its work that the WHOLE body of Christ will come to complete maturity.

Questions to Ponder...

1. What stage of growth am I currently in right now?

2. How can I encourage others in different stages than myself?

Day 11

Do not love the world or anything in the world. If anyone loves the world, the love of the Father is not in him. Everything in the world: the desires of the flesh, the desires of the eyes and the proud boasting of what one has and does, comes not from the Father, but from the world. The world and its desires are passing away, but the man who is doing the will of God is abiding forever. (1 John 2:15-17)

Origins are of great importance in how we live our lives. The question of where do our desires and pursuits come from is of utmost importance. Our actions are simply an outpouring of what is in our hearts and what we love in our hearts indicates the origin of our actions. John speaks of one of these origins when he instructs us not to love the world or anything in the world. However, this poses a great question that several seekers of God have answered wrongly. This question is: what is the world?

There are so many differing perspectives of what the world is that by going and visiting different seekers of God, one can find vastly different lifestyles. The Amish believe that things outside of their communities are the world and therefore they separated themselves from most of society. While liberal groups often feel that only gross sins constitute the world and therefore, they embrace everything in culture. These two are extreme examples, but most people fall somewhere between the two. Nevertheless, even the middle ground does not necessarily catch the heart of what John is trying to communicate in verses 16 and 17.

John describes the world as the desires of our natural being, the desires of our eyes, and the pride we have in possessions and accomplishments. He sums up this definition by defining the world as stuff that does not originate from God. There are two places in John's mind where things come from: the world or God. With this definition in mind we can see that John's concept of the world reaches far beyond any kind of external set of standards. Rather, we ourselves can be part of the world by simply operating independently of God. Are your affections for God or do you still love your possessions and comforts? If you do, you love the world and as a result you are being subtly controlled by the world.

How do we break free from the control of the world? The answer to the question is simply to do what John has said...Do Not Love The World. If you no longer allow your life to be dictated by pursuits of possessions or comforts, it will free you from the world's dominion. Instead of looking toward the things of the world, as you set the direction of your life, you must focus on the Father. Enter into fellowship with God and remain there as you consider His will. From Him comes direction and focus for our lives that will separate us from the pursuits of the world.

Do you love the world? If you do, you are not in fellowship with God and His love is not in your heart. You are on a downward spiral into the pit of hell. The world and its desires will pass away and if you love these, you will perish with them. Repent and set your hope fully upon the will of God. Seek His desires and His goals and you will experience life that is eternal.

Questions to Ponder...

1. Do I love the desires of my eyes?

2. Do I love the desires of my body?

3. Do I love to boast about earthly things that I have accomplished?

4. Did I just read the previous three questions or did I actually answer them? Is the love of the Father in me?

5. Am I doing the will of the Father or do I care more about my own desires? What does this say about my eternal state?

Day 12

Dear children, this is the last hour; and as you have heard that the antichrist is coming, even now many antichrists have come. This is how we know it is the last hour. They went out from our midst, but they were not really from us. For if they were from us, they would have continued with us; but their going showed that not all of them are from us. But you have an anointing from the Holy One, and all of you perceive the truth. I have not written to you because you do not perceive the truth, but because you do and because no lie is from the truth. Who is the liar? It is the one denying that Jesus is the Christ. Such a man is the antichrist, he denies the Father and the Son. Everyone denying the Son does not have the Father; the one agreeing with the Son has the Father also. (1 John 2:18-23)

Among those who are truly seeking Christ, there remains those who are living a lie. These people deceive themselves and others around them saying that they follow Jesus, but their actions prove differently. John writes to believers in order to confirm what they have already perceived concerning those who deny the truth pertaining to Jesus. Within these passages, John encourages them to see some things that can help us identify someone who is putting up a false front. Originally, John was likely attempting to shed light on a group of people called the Gnostics, but we need not limit his words to them alone. If someone is denying Jesus, John's words apply to them too.

Be on guard against those who believe in God and yet don't accept the man named Jesus as the Christ. Throughout the writings in the New Testament, John and other authors stress the following points. Jesus was the son of God who came to the earth in order to bring salvation to those who trust Him (John 3:16). He came to bring reconciliation between us and God through His brutal death on the cross (John 10:9-11). It is by becoming one with Jesus in His death and life that we are able to walk in fellowship with the Father (Romans 6:4-8). No one who denies Jesus Christ's death and resurrection can be reconciled into fellowship with God. Those who deny these things are antichrists (1 John 2:22).

How do you view those who deny Jesus? Do you see them as Antichrists? There are several groups today who claim to believe in God, yet deny the Son. Just to name a few would be Islam and Judaism. Both claim the same God as Christians, but both of them deny the Savior. This is no small matter, all Muslims and Jews who deny Jesus are going to hell. We all only have one hope for salvation. It is Jesus and if we deny Him, He will deny us before the Father (Matthew 10:33). Do you deny Jesus Christ? Don't forget what Paul said in Titus 1:16, *"They profess to know God, but by their actions they deny Him..."* Examine your heart and life today.

Questions to Ponder...

1. Do I pretend that those who are denying Christ Jesus by either their actions or their words have assurance before God?

2. Do any of my actions deny Jesus?

Day 13

See that what you have heard from the beginning abides in you. If what you heard from the beginning abides in you, you also will abide in the Son and in the Father. And this is what He promised us, eternal life. I have written these things to you about those who are trying to lead you astray. As for you, the anointing you received from Him abides in you, and you do not need anyone to teach you. But as His anointing teaches you about all things and as that anointing is real, and is not a counterfeit, just as it has taught you, abide in Him. And now, dear children, abide in Him, so that when He appears we may be confident and unashamed before Him at His coming. If you perceive that He is righteous, you know that everyone who is doing what is right has been born of Him. (1 John 2:24-29)

John speaks frequently about abiding or remaining in God and God abiding in us. The use of the word abide is not merely some clever term that sounds neat. Rather, it is a meticulously chosen word to bring clarity to our understanding of how we are to function as Christians.

The Greek word for abide or remain has the connotation of enduring in a certain location or condition. Therefore, John uses the word when he says, *"The slave does not remain in the house forever; the son remains forever"* (John 8: 35). In addition, Paul uses this word to say that he thinks widows would be happier if they remained unmarried (1 Corinthians 7: 40). As a result when John talks about abiding in God and God abiding in us, he is saying that we should continually exist in a certain state with God.

The state in which we are to dwell with God is described throughout 1 John. Some key words that help us to understand this state are fellowship, love, and light. When we abide in God we are in a state in which we are aware of God's thoughts and desires. What is on God's heart is illuminated unto us and we are conscious of His love toward us. This condition is not something that people are simply zapped with, but it is something that we are instructed how to enter into by the Holy Spirit. This is why John writes, *"As for you, the anointing you received from Him abides in you, and you do not need anyone to teach you. But as His anointing teaches you about all things and as that anointing is real, and is not a counterfeit, just as it has taught you, abide in Him."* (1John 2:27). This anointing is the Holy Spirit and it teaches us to abide in God.

Though the Holy Spirit is perfectly capable of teaching us to abide in God, often it takes some time for us to understand how to listen and learn from the Holy Spirit. As a result, God has given us apostles, prophets, evangelists, pastors, and teachers to help us come to this place of maturity. John was an apostle and in 1 John 2:24 he helps to direct us onto the right path when he writes, *"See that what you have heard from the beginning abides in you. If what you heard from the beginning abides in you, you also will abide in the Son and in the Father."* Nevertheless, what is it that we heard from the beginning? John tells us in the next chapter in verse 11: *"this is the message you heard from the beginning: we should love one another."* This is further expounded upon in chapter 4 verse 16 when John writes, *"And we have known and have trusted the love that God has in us. God is love, and the one abiding in love is abiding in God and God in him."* It is through our entering into a state of confidence in God's love and as a result, seeking to love others that we enter into a state of fellowship with God.

Do you abide in God? John warns and exhorts us that we should abide in God so that when He appears, we will have confidence and be unashamed before Him at His appearing. If you think that abiding in God is something that is only needful for those who are mature, then fear will grip your heart and you will be ashamed when Jesus returns. When Christ returns, He will judge men based upon if they are found to already be in Him (1 John 2:28). For all cleansing and forgiveness are for those who are walking in fellowship with God in the light. Don't let yourself be found in the same situation as those who will say, *"... Lord, Lord, did we not prophesy in your name, and cast out demons in your name, and do many mighty deeds in your name?"* Because on that day Jesus will reply to them, *"...I never knew you; depart from me, you workers of lawlessness"* (Mat 7:22-23). If you don't come to know God through abiding in Him before He returns, you never will know God.

Questions to Ponders...

1. How do I know if I am abiding in God?

2. Based upon the scripture I read today, does the Bible define me as one who abides in God?

3. Why is it important for me to strive to abide in God?

Day 14

See what sort of love the Father has given to us, that we should be called children of God; and that is what we are. The reason why the world does not know us is because it did not know Him. (1 John 3:1)

The God of the universe could love many things within His creation, but there is a special place in His heart for those who trust Him. God has so singled out those who believe that He has adopted them into His family. Consider the weight of such an action. Many of us may consider adopting a child in our lifetime, but think about who it is that God has adopted. It certainly wasn't a seemingly innocent baby just born a few days ago, but rather, a people who killed His only son. The love it has taken to cover over this offense far exceeds the depths of our imagination. Therefore, see what sort of love our Father has given that we should be called the children of God.

What is the significance that God has portrayed in the association of a father and a child to the relationship that we have entered into with Him? Undoubtedly, one could probably write volumes answering this question, but let us consider the remainder of this verse as we explore this answer. There is a special intimacy found within a healthy family. When a family isn't dysfunctional, there are close relationships between parents and children and children with siblings. The reason that these children have this close relationship is because they all share the same father. John alludes to this when he writes, *"The reason why the world does not know us is because it did not know Him."* When we come to know God as our father it brings us into intimacy and close fellowship with others who know God as their father as well.

Knowing God as our father means that we have direct access to the love He has toward us. In this relationship, we become well acquainted with how His thoughts and desires influence our lives. When walking with God, He trains each of us to live like Jesus lived on the earth. This lifestyle is so different from the way the world lives that those who don't have this relationship with the Father can't really understand and know His children. For what motivates and directs a believer's life is a mystery to unbelievers (John 3:8). Since they don't know God and His love, they can't truly know His children either.

Do your closest friends humbly walk with God knowing the depths of His love? Do you understand and relate well to people who have this relationship with God? The honest answer to these questions can shed light on where you are at with God. The reason why the world does not know the children of God is because they don't know God. If you relate to people who don't know God better than those who have close fellowship with Him, you probably don't know God. If you find yourself in this place, simply make your whole life's aim to trust God and obey Him. God will meet you where you are at and be a Father to you. Your life will be transformed and you will come to truly know the children of God.

Questions to Ponder...

1. *What people do I go to talk to when I am hurting or having difficulties in life? ...are they people who know God (i.e. they obey God's commands)?*

2. *Does my life need to change with regard to those who are my close friends? If so, what am I going to do about it?*

Day 15

My dear loved ones, now we are the children of God and what we will be has not yet been made known, but we perceive that when He appears, we will be like Him because we will see Him as He is. Everyone who has this hope in him purifies himself even as He is pure. (1 John 3:2-3)

In this world, there is much weakness and suffering. Nevertheless, our existence in this state is only temporary. Paul writes in 1 Corinthians 15:51-52, *"Behold, I tell you a mystery. We will not all sleep, but we will all be changed, in a moment, in the blinking of an eye, at the last trumpet. For the trumpet will blast, and the dead shall be raised imperishable, and we will be changed."* Paul goes on further to describe this change by writing about how we will become immortal. Immorality is known to be a characteristic of Jesus, but our transformation clearly includes even more. For John writes that what we will be has not yet been made known. Nevertheless, we do know that we will be like Jesus.

John also makes known to us a principle of transformation. This principal is that when we see Jesus, we become more like Him. Ultimately, we will one day come to see Him clearly and will become fully as He is. However, we can only currently see Jesus as a poor reflection as Paul wrote 1 Corinthians 13:12. Though the revelation of Christ will be much greater some day, this does not belittle the revelation that we already have. Paul refers to this revelation that brings about transformation when he writes, *"And we all, with unveiled faces, beholding the glory of the Lord, are being transformed into the same image from glory to glory..."* (2 Corinthians 3:18). As we come to see Christ more clearly, we are changed to become a greater display of His glory.

The changes that we experience today start from within, coming as a result of our minds being renewed (Romans 12:2). When we come to see Christ in a greater fullness, it changes our outlook on life. As we see things differently, it affects the decisions we make and the attitudes we have in the midst of our circumstances. From the inside out, we become transformed into the image of Christ so that we possess His character, wisdom, and gifting.

This transformation is by no means a passive endeavor, as if we were laying on the table while God operates on our souls. Rather, we are to deny ourselves, daily take up our cross, and follow Him (Luke 9:23). The cross is an instrument that brings brutal death and death is exactly what certain areas of our lives need. For no area in our lives should rule our attitudes and decisions, but Christ alone. Anything that rules in place of Christ in our lives must be put to death. It is through the process of identifying these things and crucifying them that we purify ourselves just as He is pure.

Are you waiting for God to purify you or are you purifying yourself as you behold His purity? Certainly, God does purify us in certain ways, but we are also active participants in this cleansing. When we are beholding God's purity, compassion, and glory, it equips us to put our natural man to death (Galatians 5:24). Don't wait for cleansing to magically happen in your life, rather hop into God's shower and start scrubbing. Just like God gave the Israelites the promised land and they had to conquer it by force, so too God has given us victory and we need to lay hold of it.

Questions to Ponder...

1. Does any area of my life need to be purified? If so, what area of my life is still dirty?

2. What do I specifically need to do to purify the areas of my life that aren't as pure as Jesus?

Day 16

Everyone who is sinning is also doing lawlessness and sin is lawlessness. You know that He appeared to take away our sins, and in Him there is no sin. The one abiding in Him is not sinning; the one who is sinning has neither seen Him nor known Him. (1 John 3:4-6)

There are many different perspectives about what sin is and when people don't realize this fact confusion often arises. Some people view sin as a mistake or error. They see it as simply not fully meeting up to the standard of perfection. Others view sin as rebellion and willful disregard of God's instructions. There were even some in John's day named the Gnostics who had a totally differently perspective. *"...In Gnosticism, sin...is not the act and the disposition of the human will in rebellion against God; it is only a physical fact or quality inherent in the body and in matter everywhere"* ("Gnosticism", International Standard Bible Encyclopedia). With all these perspectives of sin, John needed to clearly identify what kind of "sin" he was addressing before he began his important instruction on the topic. As a result, he wrote, *"sin is lawlessness."*

The word lawlessness is primarily a general term for rebellion and wickedness. This can be seen most clearly by observing this Greek word's usage in the Septuagint. The Septuagint is an ancient translation of the Hebrew Old Testament into Greek. When the Greek word for Lawlessness is used in the Septuagint, it is translated from nearly 20 different words all meaning something like rebellion, wickedness, and vanity *see footnote*[1]. As

---

1   See the following Strong's Numbers for the Hebrew words translated Lawlessness in the Septuagint: H5771, H205, H8441, H1100, H1892,

a result, when John writes that sin is lawlessness, he is communicating that this sin is not merely simple mistakes nor some inert quality of physical matter, but rather, rebellion against God.

Understanding that John is speaking about rebellion and wickedness can keep us from misinterpreting what he was communicating when he writes: *"The one abiding in Him is not sinning; the one who is sinning has neither seen Him nor known Him."* This does not read that those abiding in God are sinlessly perfect, but that those who abide in Him don't continue in blatant rebellion against Him. Abiding in God has a powerful effect on our lives and it enables us to take dominion over strongholds. This dominion is won through special insight into our weakness, discipline, and positive reinforcement. Just as parents train their children, God trains us when we abide in Him.

It is for this reason that Jesus came into the world, that he might take away our sins. Jesus brought reconciliation with God so that we might know God as our father. With God as our father training us there is no way that we can continue to walk in wickedness. Examine yourself to see if any sin has continued to persist in your life over the years and take John's words to heart: *"The one abiding in Him is not sinning; the one who is sinning has neither seen Him nor known Him"* (1 John 3:6).

Question to Ponder...

1. Am I lawless?

2. Does John think that I know God?

H1942, H2555, H2930, H4604, H5627, H5766, H6090, H6588, H7562

Day 17

Dear children, do not let anyone deceive you. He who is doing what is right is righteous, just as he is righteous. He who is doing what is sinful is of the devil, because the devil has been sinning from the beginning. The reason the Son of God appeared was to destroy the devil's work. Everyone having been born of God will not continue to sin, because God's seed remains in him; he is not able to go on sinning, because he has been born of God. (1 John 3:7-9)

A great deception reigns in much of Christendom these days. Many church members think that their wicked lifestyle is something that everyone will have to bear with until the day of their death. Countless millions have fallen into this deception thinking that God is going to overlook their continuing wickedness and has accepted them as His children. Nevertheless, John speaks against this deception when he declares that it is those who do what is right that are right with God. Those who are rebelling are not children of God, but are children of the Devil.

The Devil is a great deceiver and in these last days many people are seeking teachers who will tell them that they can live however they want and still be right with God (2 Timothy 4:3). Some of these deceivers tell us that we can pursue prosperity in life and still walk with God. However, those who make it their aim to accumulate wealth will be judged among the wicked (Luke 12:15-34). Other's say that sexual relationships outside of marriage are acceptable before God, but in reality Paul warns us that those who live like this won't enter the kingdom of heaven (Galatians 5:19-21). In addition, there are teachers who will say that God doesn't care if we watch movies full of violence and sexual immorality. Nevertheless, God hates violence and all other sin (Psalm 11:5, Ezekiel 33:11). If we think we can entertain ourselves with the bile of the world, then we are an enemy of God (James 4:4). God has called His people to be set apart, but if we still take pleasure in things God hates, a deeper problem lies at our inner root.

When John speaks of people not continuing in sin, the reason he gives is based upon an inner work. This work is that of a birth into life with God: the fusion of God's genes into our spirit. This means that the nature of God's heart has been sparked to life within us. When this happens it begins the process of transformation where we go from desiring self pleasure to desiring God's pleasure. As this change takes place within us, we become repulsed by wickedness and sin. When God's nature is continually growing within us there comes a point where sinful practices in our lives will cease because we can no longer tolerate them anymore.

You may have something in your life that you know is wrong and you hate it, but its hold on you seems impossible to break. Don't take comfort saying to yourself, *"I am just young in the Lord and haven't gotten to that place of maturity yet."* Rather consider your life and where you invest your time. Paul reminds us in Galatians 6:8 that where we invest our time will be reflected in the fruit of our lives: *"The one who sows to please his earthly nature, from that nature will reap destruction; the one who sows to please the Spirit, from the Spirit will reap eternal life."* As a result, if you find that the sin in your life has too great of a hold on you, it is time to change what you are feeding into your life. The seed of God will not grow in hard, rocky, and weedy soil (Mark 4:15-20). Dig deep into your life and cut off everything that hinders. Pursue moment by moment fellowship with God and sin will loosen its grip on your heart.

Questions to Ponder...

1. Am I in bondage to any specific sin? If so, do I hate it?

2. Am I willing to stop doing things that are planting bad seeds in my heart?

3. What kind of seeds am I planting into my heart by the things I participate in? ...are there any bad seeds?

4. When I read what John has written, does it produce confidence in my heart that I have been born of God? If not, am I going to take what he writes seriously?

Day 18

By this it is evident who are the children of God, and who are the children of the devil: everyone who is not doing righteousness is not from God, nor is the one not loving his brother. This is the message you heard from the beginning: We should love one another, unlike Cain, who belonged to the evil one and murdered his brother. And why did he murder him? Because his own actions were evil and his brother's were righteous. Do not be surprised, my brothers, if the world hates you. We know that we have passed from death to life, because we love our brothers. Anyone who does not love remains in death. Everyone who hates his brother is a murderer, and you know that no murderer has eternal life abiding in him. (1 John 3:10-15)

Paul elevates three virtues above the rest in 1 Corinthians 13:13 when he writes, *"And now these three are remaining: faith, hope and love. But the greatest of these is love."* Nothing is more pivotal in the Christian life than love. John teaches us from his first letter that it is the defining mark which distinguishes believers from the world. If people don't love, they are neither children of God nor do they have eternal life in them. On the other hand, all who seek to know God will learn to walk in love as they find Him.

What is this love and why is it so distinguishing from other virtues? People can do things for all sorts of reasons. Many give to charities because it gives them a tax break at the end of the year and it puts them in good standing with nonprofit organizations. Nevertheless, they don't actually possess the tender care and supreme value for the hurting and needy to which the organization is helping. They simply contribute the money because they need to and because it makes them look good. This is different from love. Love is not self seeking, but rather places its value on others. Love shows kindness out of a response of care and value placed on others, instead of extending kindness for personal gain. This greatly separates Christians from the world because only true love exists in a heart touched by God.

The origin of Christian love comes neither through other people nor from a disciplined lifestyle, but by the filling of the Holy Spirit (Romans 5:5). This love is experienced through the testimony that God gives us by the Spirit: *"The Spirit Himself testifies with our spirit that we are God's children"* (Romans 8:16). Such a testimony is an incomprehensible expression of love, just as John writes earlier in chapter 3, *"See what sort of love the Father has given to us, that we should be called children of God"* (1 John 3:1). It is this inner testimony that is the origin of the continual care and supreme value that the children of God possess. When people don't know this testimony, the expression of their life displays an absence of true love. John calls these people dead and explains that they don't have eternal life abiding in them.

Though death is in the absence of Love, eternal life is in the presence of it. Few Christians really see eternal life as the opposite of being spiritually dead. Rather, they view eternal life as never going to hell. Such people don't quite understand John's perspective on these matters. In his gospel, John quotes Jesus saying, *"Now this is eternal life: that they may know you, the only true God, and Jesus Christ, whom you have sent"* (John 17:3). Therefore, eternal life is experienced when believers are conscious of God's fatherly love. For, God is love and whoever abides in love abides in God. In this way, those who come to know God, come to know His love. The overflow of God's love in people's lives is the fruit that bears testimony that they have passed from death to life (1 John 3:14).

What is the fruit of your life? Is your heart full of care and concern for others or are you primarily focused on yourself? Do you rest in confidence with God or is your life an expression of fear and insecurity? Love is not self seeking and if you are frequently looking to get something for yourself when you are kind to others, you may not even know what love really is. If your life contains defensive outbursts of anger, depression, and or pursuits of privacy you likely suffer from fear and insecurity. If your life is full of fear, insecurity, and selfish ambition you are not walking in God's love and you're dead. Fear, insecurity, and self seeking motives stem from not experiencing God's inner testimony of love. You may read the Bible, pray, and go to church, but if you're not conscious of God's love, you don't know Him. God is love and he desires that you would surrender all your ambitions and pursuits to Him. Make it your goal to trust Him in every way, yielding your perspectives and actions to the teachings of the Bible, and when you persevere in these, you will find eternal life.

Questions to Ponder...

1. Do I have self seeking motives when I do nice things for others?

2. What would real love for others look like in my life?

3. According to what John wrote, have I passed from death to life?

Day 19

This is the message you heard from the beginning: we should love one another, unlike Cain, who belonged to the evil one and murdered his brother. And why did he murder him? Because his own actions were evil and his brother's were righteous. Do not be surprised, my brothers, if the world hates you. (1 John 3:11-13)

Those who dwell in the darkness of the world, like to believe that they are ultimately good and that they will one day go to heaven. Nevertheless, God does not have fellowship with everyone and one day He will send those who live for themselves to Hell. These evil people have dulled their consciences and have justified their sin, so that only when someone who walks in true righteousness comes near to these rebels does the reality of their state become evident. When these sinners are faced with the reality of who they are, their anger and hatred usually becomes focused on those who exposed them. Such people's hatred inspires them to snuff out the light of the righteous ones who have loved them most.

Cain sought to snuff out the light that exposed his wickedness when he hated and murdered his brother Abel. In the same way, many of the prophets of the Old Testament forfeited their lives to speak the truth to the Israelites who desired to remain in darkness. Likewise, if we live righteously and speak the truth, we will face persecution: *"Because it has been given unto you for Christ's sake, not only to trust Him, but also to suffer for Him"* (Philippians 1:29). Christ suffered on the earth and He explained that we would suffer too. In John 15:19, Jesus said, *"if you were from the world, it would affectionately love you. This is why the world hates you: because you are not from the world, but I have chosen you out of the world,"* then later He adds, *"...if they persecuted me, they will persecute you also..."* (John 15:20). It should be no surprise to find that the world hates the true followers of Christ Jesus because it hates Jesus.

In John 7:7, Jesus explained why the world hated Him: *"the world is not able to hate you, but it hates me, because I testify concerning it, that its works are evil."* Jesus was a faithful witness to the things He observed and He didn't water down sin. In deep care and honesty, Jesus rebuked all forms of sin without concern for the offense it might cause. Those who repented, He called His 'friends' (John 15:15), but those who arrogantly opposed Him He called 'hypocrites', 'whitewashed tombs', and 'snakes' (Matthew 23:27, 33). The words of Jesus can be quite severe and sharp like a double edged sword, nevertheless in the midst of these rebukes His heart was gentle and lowly (Matthew 11:29).

Many people, attempting to mimic Jesus' severity, have done so without possessing His heart. Such people receive persecution and suffer for the things they say and do. Nevertheless, these people are not really suffering for the name of Christ, but because they are rude or obnoxious. When people try to speak with Jesus' severity, but don't possess the deep care and love for the ones they are speaking to, their message is only a resounding gong or a clanging symbol (1 Corinthians 13:1). Such people are more concerned about speaking what they believe and showing that others are wrong than reconciling sinners to a holy God. Paul addressed this wrong attitude when he wrote, *"...avoid foolish and undisciplined disputes, seeing that they breed quarrels. The servant of the Lord does not need to quarrel, but to be mild to all, able to teach, enduring evil, and to chasten his opponents in gentleness. Perhaps then God will give them repentance unto a full knowledge of the truth and they will regain their senses from the snare of the Devil who has taken them captive to do his will"* (2 Timothy 2:23-26). Those who inappropriately correct others are acting no more like Jesus than the ones they reprove.

Though Jesus' reproof of the proud could be quite severe, it was rooted in the hope that His hearers would be reconciled to God. This can be seen in one of Jesus' most lengthy and extreme rebukes to the Pharisees. In Matthew 23, Jesus severely chastens the Pharisees and then concludes with these pleading words: *"Jerusalem, Jerusalem, the one killing the prophets and throwing stones at the ones sent to her. How often, I have desired to gather together your children as a hen gathers her chicks under her wings and you were not willing"* (Matthew 23:37). Though Jesus used severe and sharp words, His longing desire was to cut people off from the world and unite them to the Father before they face the Day of Judgement.

The Father has deeply loved the world and does not desire to see anyone perish, but to have all come to repentance (2 Peter 3:9). If you possess the same love that God has for sinners, you will find yourself warning them that God will judge their evil works. Even your life will illuminate their condemnation and those who refuse to repent will hate you. Nevertheless, as you live in this world remember these words: *"but even if you should suffer on account of righteousness, you are blessed. You should not fear what they fear nor should you be troubled. Set apart Christ as Lord in your heart and always be prepared to answer everyone who asks you the reason for the hope that is in you, but do this with gentleness and respect, having a good conscience. Do this so that when you are spoken against, those who accuse you may be put to shame by your good conduct in Christ. It is better to suffer for doing good, if it is God's will than to do evil"* (1 Peter 3:14-17)

Question to Ponder

Do I suffer persecution? ...why?

Day 20

This is how we know what love is: Jesus Christ laid down His life for us. And we ought to lay down our lives for our brothers. (1 John 3:16)

People have so many definitions of love in the world and because each of us started out in the world, we must examine our own definition. In the world, love can mean anything from having sex with someone to a person's enjoyment of ice cream. Nevertheless, the world knows nothing about true love. Rather, its definitions of love are mere imitations of the glorious reality. Only that which is perfect can truly be an example of perfect love. In this way, Jesus was the only one who could truly introduce us to the fullness of love available through the Holy Spirit.

When John writes that we have come to know what love is by seeing how Jesus laid down his life. He is not simply referring to Christ's physical death. There are a couple different words for life in the Greek language and John did not choose the word for life here that would mean the breathing vitality of a person. Instead, he chose the word for life that refers to the summation of one's being. In other passages this word is translated *"soul."* This helps us to understand that we come to know what love is by seeing how Jesus sacrificed His whole being.

In Philippians 2:8, Paul writes about the sacrifices Jesus made: *"Who, being in the very nature God, did not consider equality with God as an achievement to be held onto, but made Himself nothing, taking the very nature of a servant, being made in human likeness. And being found in appearance as a man, He humbled Himself and became obedient to death-- even death on a cross!"* This description of Jesus' sacrifice can be summed up in that He did not look out for His own interests, but also for the interests of others. His love can be seen in His willingness to become a servant, subject to human weakness. Even though He possessed the glory of God, He did not consider it of greater value than reconciling us to Himself and having spiritual fellowship with us. He laid down His very being to the fullest measure, totally giving Himself up as a sacrifice that we might come to know the true meaning of love and be saved.

Jesus didn't teach us what love is, simply to enjoy it by ourselves. He taught us the meaning of love so that we might share its riches with others. In the same way that Jesus gave up His very being, we too are to fully give up ourselves for others. Are you willing to give up your dignity and image before the world in order to care about others? God is calling you to, but not to do it grudgingly. For those who make sacrifices without joy are simply exercising their duty, rather than sharing the love they have received from God. God does not want your carnal attempts to obey His command to love. He wants you to experience His love and to share it with others. If you find yourself not having love well up out of your heart for others, stop and consider again what Jesus has done and offer up thanksgiving to Him. From your thankful heart will spring the love you desire to reflect.

Questions to Ponder...

1. How do I define love? ...does my perspective match John's?

2. In what ways did Jesus lay down His existence for me?

3. How should I lay down my very being for others?

Day 21

If anyone has material possessions and sees his brother in need, but closes his heart to him, how can the love of God be in him? Dear children, let us not love with words or tongue but with actions and in truth. In this, we know that we belong to the truth, and we persuade our hearts in His presence. Because, if our hearts condemn us, God is greater than our hearts, and He knows everything. Dear loved ones, if our hearts do not condemn us, we have confidence before God and receive from Him whatever we ask, because we keep His commands and do what pleases Him.
(1 John 3:17-22)

Various Christian groups and denominations seek to find assurance of their salvation and standing before God on several different grounds. Some believe assurance is obtained by placing confidence in saying a prayer to God that they are sorry for their past actions and that they *"accept Jesus into their heart."* Others find assurance by rigorous study and basing their confidence in the conclusions they deduce from their academic work. Though people can place their confidence in all sorts of things, John tells us that our confidence is directly related to the fruit coming from our lives.

Great concern often arises when people begin examining the fruit coming from their lives, because many condemn themselves by how they live. A man will view a bunch of pornography. Then later, sit down to enjoy a brutally violent movie and still profess to be following Jesus in right standing with Him. When people don't see their actions as evidence of how they are relating to God, they can't see the contradiction in their lives. John closely ties our actions to our relationship with God to show us that there is no assurance for those who remain selfish and wicked.

Selfishness and wickedness are bound deeply in the heart of men and it is a life long process to drive them out. Nevertheless, assurance exists for those who are driving these things out. In verse seventeen of this chapter, John doesn't merely question someone's actions when they don't help those in need, but rather he questions what is in their heart. If God's love is present within a person's inner being, it will continually work to transform the outside of their being. Therefore, John teaches us that if the work of God's love is not affecting our outward actions, God's love is not present inside our hearts.

True assurance arises out of the work of God's love within us. In 1 John 4:18, we read, *"There is no fear in love, but matured love casts out fear because fear has torment and the one who is fearful has not been matured in love."* Assurance is found in the absence of fear and as John teaches: it is in the presence of God's perfect love that fear is cast out. If God's love does not exist in our hearts, we will either constantly be questioning and condemning ourselves or we will live in wickedness with a seared conscience. John, hoping to eliminate these possibilities, exhorts us to listen to our hearts and examine the fruit coming from our lives. God who knows all things will not judge us based upon our ignorance in these matters. Therefore, let us be diligent to be found spotless, blameless and at peace with Him in our hearts (2 Peter 3:14). Then we will naturally possess assurance that we are experiencing real Christianity (1 John 3:21-22).

Are you experiencing real Christianity, walking in a right standing with God or does your life and your heart condemn you? A peace that transcends all understanding exists for those walking with God (Philippians 4:6-9) . If you are not experiencing this peace, you need to change. Your ambitions, where you place your confidence, and your willingness to lay down your life for others must come under submission to Jesus. Cast yourself before the one who knows all things without justifying your failures. Believe and trust in His love and it will penetrate your heart. Offer up thanksgiving to God and turn away from vanity. True life and assurance can be placed within you, if only you will pursue Him with all your heart.

Questions to Ponder...

1. Where do I find assurance before God? Does this match with what John has written?

2. Who does God give peace and assurance to?

Day 22

And this is His command: to trust in the name of His Son, Jesus Christ, and to love one another as He has commanded us. Those who are keeping His commands are abiding in Him, and He in them. And in this we know that He abides in us: by the Spirit He gave us. (1 John 3:23-24)

When some people think of obedience to God's commands their minds start making associations with legalism, tyranny, bondage, and the Old Testament. Nevertheless, all these are far from what John has been writing about in the last couple chapters. In this passage, the substance of God's commands are explained as trusting Jesus and loving others. These instructions are so pivotal to the Christian life that obedience to them is considered an indication of God's abiding presence.

Though love and trust naturally result when abiding in God's presence, they are still commands that must be obeyed. These commands are the gateway and condition for continuing in close fellowship with God. Our fellowship with God begins on the basis of us placing our confidence in Him. Paul writes in several places how it is through trusting that we gain access to the favor of God's presence (Romans 5:2, Ephesians 2:8, Colossians 2:12). If we don't obey the command to believe and trust in Jesus we cannot come to know God. Likewise, we cannot continue to walk with God unless we obey His command to love. God has shown us an infinite measure of love in reconciling us to Himself and if we don't express the same compassion toward others, He will not continue to show us His compassion (Matthew 18:23-35). Therefore, walking with God demands that we obey

His command to trust Him and love others.

God has not expected us to obey His command to trust and love without help. Rather, He is meticulously drawing us to Himself through circumstances, people, spiritual forces, the scriptures, and especially His own son. Even before we ever loved or trusted God, He demonstrated His own love for us in that while we were still sinners, He sacrificed His only son on our behalf (Romans 8:8). God did this so that we might believe that He truly loves us and therefore trust Him. When we trust and place our confidence in His love, it opens the door to His empowering presence in our lives (Romans 5:2). In His presence, there is fullness of joy and obedience to His commands are not burdensome. Though we must yield our hearts to Him, He is constantly working to motivate our desires and actions toward pursuit of His joy (Philippians 2:13).

God's joy, along with our obedience to trust and love, can grant us great confidence that the Holy Spirit is abiding in us. Paul speaks of these assuring qualities when he writes, *"...the fruit of the Spirit is love, joy, peace, patience, kindness, goodness, trust, gentleness and self control..."* (Galatians 5:22-23). We know the presence of God's Spirit in our lives when its fruit is ripening in our hearts. This means that our confidence of God's indwelling is that there is supernatural love, joy, peace, self control etc. coming out of our being. This is why John writes, *"And in this we know that He abides in us: by the Spirit He gave us."* If the fruit of our lives does not come from the Holy Spirit, it is time to question whether God's Spirit is really dwelling within us.

What is coming out of your heart? Are you patient with others, consistently exercising self control when tempted? Does the fruit of the Spirit confirm God's presence in your heart? If not, fix your eyes on Jesus. His great power brought all of creation into existence. He knows the secrets within everyone's heart. He endured the cross and sacrificed His whole being because He loves you. You can trust Him! Place your confidence in Him, with regard to every aspect of your life. When you experience His merciful love, share it with others. Share it not only with those who are kind to you, but also to your enemies. For, those who obey His commands abide in Him and He in them. The abundance of God's riches in Christ Jesus await you.

Questions to Ponder...

1. Do I obey God's commands?

2. What kind of fruit is coming out of my heart?

Day 23

My dear loved ones, do not trust every spirit, but test the spirits to see if they are from God because many false prophets have gone out into the world. This is how we know the spirit that is from God, every spirit that agrees that Jesus Christ has come in the flesh is from God. Every spirit that does not agree with Jesus is not from God, this is the spirit that is from the Antichrist which you heard is coming and is already in the world. (1 John 4:1-3)

When people think of the Antichrist, they often think of some man who will come at the end of the age and will unite the world against God. They think of the great tribulation, a seven year period, and persecution of God's people. Such thoughts about the Antichrist are misplaced here. For John tells us that the Antichrist has already been in the world for nearly two thousand years. John is not trying to expound upon some end times leader, but rather he is identifying the source from which some spirits speak.

The word spirit holds many different connotations to the average person. At times, it is another word for a ghost (that is a dead person). Other times it is an angel or a demon. Sometimes it can be an attitude that a person expresses. Nevertheless, John is primarily using this word to describe the rational part of a human being. This can be observed when he writes, *"because many false prophets have gone out into the world."* A prophet is a person who receives a message and passes it along to others. John teaches his readers here how to discern where a prophet's message originates. He explains that there are two places where a prophet's words can come from: God or the Antichrist. People who speak from God tell the truth, but those who are of the Antichrist are liars who oppose Jesus Christ.

In the past, the people John was against were likely the Gnostics. This group of people claimed that Jesus Christ did not come in the flesh. Instead of saying that Jesus was a real man, they claimed that he was some kind of spiritual being who never really suffered, died, and rose again. These people denied the very things that Jesus said about himself. Jesus claimed to be the son of man (a real human) throughout the gospels (Matthew 12:40, Mark 8:31, Luke 22:48, John 6:27) and Revelation 1:18 emphatically states that He died and rose to life. The Gnostics' disregard for Jesus' own teaching about Himself indicates that they were not speaking from God; rather, they were speaking from the Antichrist. John wanted his readers not to be led astray from God by these Gnostics.

John's intent for his readers to be on guard was certainly not limited to the Gnostics, for he does not name them specifically, but rather gives us a principle to teach us to discern everyone who speaks from the Antichrist. This principle is that everyone who does not agree with Jesus is not from God. When so called Christian leaders today do not teach the same things Jesus taught, they are speaking from the Antichrist. In Luke 14:33, Jesus teaches us that we cannot be a follower of Him unless we surrender every aspect of our lives to Him. However, those who speak from the Antichrist have taught a widely accepted deception today that people can say a simple prayer once in life, virtually live however they want, and go to heaven. If we are not familiar with the truth written in the Bible, we will be tricked by these spirits of deception.

Do you diligently study the Bible? Many people who view themselves as Christians have so little knowledge of the actual words written in the Bible that they are being deceived by the spirits of the Antichrist. There will come a day when the Man of Lawlessness will appear and he will deceive the world through signs and wonders. If you are already being deceived by the Antichrist's prophets, when the Antichrist himself comes, you will most certainly be led astray. For if you don't love the truth enough now to diligently become established in it, God will hand you over to the powerful delusion that is to come (2 Thessalonians 2:7-12). No excuse exists before God on the Day of Judgment for those, who due to their laziness, were unable to test the spirits and see if they were from God.

Questions to Ponder...

1. What are the three things that I spend the most time listening, watching, or reading?

2. Do the people and things I listen to agree with Jesus? If not, who or what do I need to stop listening to?

3. Do I know of any people or things that do agree with Jesus? If yes, what can I do to be more blessed by these?

Day 24

You are from God, dear children, and have overcome them, because greater is the one who is in you than the one who is in the world. (1 John 4:4)

Many Christians have heard the phrase, *"Greater is He who is in you, than he who is in the world."* Nevertheless, most people are not familiar with the first half of this verse. For John says that we who are from God have overcome them, but who are *"them"* that we overcome? By looking into the context of this passage we find that *"them"* are the spirits who are from the Antichrist. The spirits who are from the Antichrist are the false prophets that are leading the world astray. Therefore, we who are from God, have power to overcome these spirits because the one who is in us is greater than the one who is in the world.

The Devil is prowling around ready to come against those of us who are seeking God. Just like he was present when Jesus was being tested in the desert, so too the Devil, his demons, and those who are speaking for the Antichrist, are near us in our time of testing. They come in the form of dreams, thoughts, and people. Approaching us when we are tired and weak, they plant doubts and lies in our minds to steer us away from the truth. If we listen to such deceivers, they will direct us away from life in fellowship with God.

Beware of such deceivers, for they say: *"You can't keep overcoming, eventually you are going to get too weak and fail." "Your sin isn't that bad, you just can't help it." "It's just too much, you have to give in." "You don't deserve to be treated that way and they deserve what you did to them." "Things in your life are never going to change; you might as well give up." "Just a little won't hurt, you'll be fine." "If you do it, your desire will be satisfied.*" "*How bad is this thing?*" "*Everyone is doing it...*" "*What are people going to think about you?*" "*You would be so much happier if you had that too.*" "*You'll feel a lot better by making them pay for what they did to you.*" "*No one will know.*" "*Who cares, it doesn't matter, just do it.*" "*You will always burn inside until you do it.*" "*What if...what if...what if...*" "*It's hopeless.*" "*No one understands.*" "*You are a child of God, go for it, you surely won't die...*" The Devil uses these words by speaking them into our thoughts by demons and speaking them into our ears by people. These are the ones whom John tells us we can overcome.

We can overcome those who lie to us because He who is in us is greater than the deceiver of the world. In what way is He greater? The Devil's deceptive darkness cannot overcome the light of God's truth within us. No matter how many lies the Devil can speak through his servants, God can speak more truth to us. For every lie we hear, we can also hear truth from God to keep us in the way we should go. The question is then, who are we listening to? If we start listening to the Devil and stop listening to God then the Devil's lies will lead us astray. Nevertheless, if we follow Jesus' example by rejecting all lies from the Devil and only accepting the truth from God, there is no way that we can be overcome. Just as Jesus said, "*If you abide in my word, you are truly my disciples, and you will know the truth, and the truth will set you free*" (John 8:31-32).

Questions to Ponder...

1. What lies do I most often hear?

2. What truth contradicts the lies I hear most?

Day 25

They are from the world and therefore speak from the world, and the world listens to them. We are from God, and those who know God listen to us. Those who are not from God do not listen to us, from this we know the spirit of truth and the spirit of deception.
(1 John 4:5-6)

False teachers and prophets are everywhere today in the world in which we live. Nevertheless, these people do not openly identify themselves as such. As a result, many people have no idea who they are. These false prophets and teachers give guidance and direction to what they believe is meaningful in life and what really matters. Unfortunately, they are not instructing people with words from God, but words from the Devil and the world. If we are going to please God and walk with Him we must learn to identify those who will lead us astray and those who will lead us into truth.

One major key to identifying if someone is of the spirit of truth or the spirit of deception is to see who is listening to them. John tells us that the world listens to those who are of the world and we know from Paul that the way of this world is in accord with the deceptive spirit at work in those who are disobedient (Ephesians 2:2). Therefore, when we see those who are of the world listening and following someone or something we must beware. This is not to say that just because unbelievers enjoy something that it is inherently wrong, but rather that we should examine these things to see if they are pleasing to God (1 Corinthians 6:12, 10:23).

The people of this world are pleased by all kinds of things that God hates. From Psalms 11:5 we know that God hates those who enjoy violence and yet, Hollywood regularly portrays violence as exciting and fun to watch. In addition, many movies today instruct their viewers that sex before marriage is great; while on the other hand, God calls it sexual immorality and says that those who continue in it are going to hell (Galatians 5:19-21). Though our movies today do not call themselves false prophets and teachers, they are speaking and teaching us things from the world and the spirit of deception. It is their message that the world is listening to and those who are following their instructions don't heed the words of the Bible.

When people are not heeding the words of the Bible they are following the ways of the Antichrist, for he is anti-Christian: he is against the values and perceptions of Christ Jesus. Those who are not from God teach not only gross denials of Jesus' words, they also promote subtle diversions from His ways. Such diversions may include: worrying about the necessities of life (Matthew 6:25-34), constantly desiring the next new greatest thing on the market (Luke 12:15), and boastfully trying to become famous and receive recognition (Matthew 6:2). The greatest promoters of these things today are often television commercials. No matter what people watch on TV, whether it is the news, a sporting event, or a sitcom, they all are littered with commercials that seek to draw people's hearts away from God. These commercials are some of the Devil's greatest spokesmen (prophets). Their subtlety and cleverness captures the attention and heart of those who would never purposefully sit down to watch them. They weasel their way into homes and seduce children, women, and men. Yet few people are willing to turn off this source of corruption because they love the shows that are on in between airing of these false prophets.

Many will allow themselves to be seduced for hours before this corruption and will barely open their Bibles to bring themselves to purity. John says that those who know God listen to the writers of the Bible and those who are not from God don't. If you think that it is fine to fill your mind with the things spoken from the Spirit of this World, beware lest you find yourself judged as corrupt on the Day of Judgment. For Paul warns us when he wrote, *"Do not be deceived: God cannot be mocked. A man reaps what he sows. The one who sows to please his earthly nature, from that nature will reap destruction; the one who sows to please the Spirit, from the Spirit will reap eternal life"* (Galatians 6:7-8). If you are from God, you will be listening to His spokesmen and they will guide you into fellowship with the Father. Examine the influences in your life and guard your heart against today's false prophets.

Questions to Ponder...

1. Do I follow after things that people who don't know God pursue?

2. Do I regularly hear the Devils prophets speaking? If yes, why do I let them try their best to lead me astray?

3. What can I do to keep myself from being tricked by the Devil's spokesmen?

Day 26

Dear loved ones, let us love one another, for love comes from God. Everyone who loves has been born of God and knows God. Whoever does not love does not know God, because God is love. (1 John 4:7-8)

In America, many people profess to be Christians, but only a few of these actually know God. The most evident quality that shows their hypocrisy is that they don't possess true love. If people truly loved they would be like God, for God is love. When people walk with God and experience fellowship with Him, they learn what true love really is, because they see love demonstrated toward them in their daily life. Unfortunately, many people never walk in this relationship with God. Such people are in a terrible situation, because only God can perfectly demonstrate love and only He can truly expose the deep misunderstandings in our hearts. If we want to obey God's command to love one another, we must come to know Him, because love comes from God and God Himself is love.

Paul refers to this direct instruction from God to learn to walk in love when he writes, *"Now concerning brotherly love we do not need to write to you, for you yourselves have been taught by God to love each other"* (1 Thessalonians 4:9). God is the best father who loves us more perfectly than any human ever could. In the same way that we are able to get to know our earthly father, we are able to experience and know our heavenly father. He is able to tell us that He loves us, correct us when we are wrong, and guide us into the right way. One way God does this is through His Holy Spirit who dwells within us: *"But the Counselor, the Holy Spirit, whom the Father will send in my name, He will teach you all things and will remind you of everything I have said to you"* (John 14:26) (see also Romans 5:5, Titus 3:4-5). It is this intimate connection with God through the Holy Spirit that marks the difference between those who have been born again and those who have not (John 3:3-8).

This spiritual interaction with God is dominated by the essence and character of God Himself. Just as John has said, *"God is love,"* so everything that comes from interacting with God is rooted in this quality. Nevertheless, the world has twisted the meaning of love to divert our attention from its reality. Thankfully, God has preserved for us a witness to help us to identify the love we receive through the Holy Spirit when we experience it. This witness is the Bible. 1 Corinthians 13 explains to us that love is patient, kind, humble, not easily angered, and hopeful. Proverbs teaches us that love brings correction and discipline to guide others in the right way (Proverbs 3:11-12; 13:24). John 15:13 instructs us that love is self sacrificing. When we enter the presence of God, we become aware of these qualities of love in their purist state. Those who have not come to know these qualities do not know God, because God is love.

Though we can all experience God's love through other Spirit filled people, only a personal connection with God will ultimately enlighten us to know how to love others. Do you know God's love through the Holy Spirit or is your Christian walk more oriented toward the outward experience of love from other people? Certainly, human interaction is important to the Christian life, but ultimately your interaction with other believers should be helping you come to know God personally through the Holy Spirit. If you have not yet come to know God's love, you need to start to trust the things He says. Believe and meditate upon God's words with a humble heart and you will come to know love by the Holy Spirit.

Questions to Ponder...

1. *Where did I get my definition of love? Is it the same as John's definition?*

2. *Have I experience God's love for me? ...do I live like I am depended on God's love?*

3. *Do I love others with the same kind of love that God has loved me? ...why?*

Day 27

*This is how God's love was displayed among us,
God sent His only begotten son into the world
that we might become alive through Him. In
this is love, not that we have loved God, but that
He has loved us and sent His son to be the one
who satisfied the judgment on account of our sins.
(1 John 4:9-10)*

Many of us have heard that Jesus died for us, but a significant portion of us know this only as information. Just as any other notable fact that we have come to learn, Jesus' death can become categorized with other historical events. It can seem so distant in the past that we forget about the significance of what God did in order to reconcile us with Himself. God loved us so much that He sent His son into the world that we might not destroy ourselves in our rebellion, but have life forever in our fellowship with Him. It is this self sacrificing act and its result that teaches us that God loves us.

The sacrifice of those dearest to us causes great pain. In the same way, God endured great pain in order to keep us from facing the punishment that we were destined for. Jesus is described as God's only begotten son. He would then be God's heir and one to whom He would give all that He has. Jesus was God's little boy. The one who He could hold up, look into His eyes, and think, this one is made out of me. Jesus was the one whom He trained and raised for 30 years on the earth and poured everything He had into Him. This Jesus was the one whom God sacrificed for us. He was God's best, His only son, and the accumulation of all His work. God gave it all. He sacrificed all that was His in order to keep us from getting what we deserve. When we consider what God went through by sacrificing His son, it gives us a deeper understanding of God's love.

If all that He went through in sacrificing His son was not enough, John adds that God sent His son for those who have not deserved it. For he writes, *"In this is love, not that we have loved God, but that He has loved us…"* The word 'loved' when John writes, *"not that we have loved God,"* is found in a special Greek tense known as the perfect tense. This means that John is saying that we have not loved God in such a way that it has had a lasting effect to cause Him to do something for us; rather, John is saying that God loved us apart from anything we had done. For John chose a different tense to describe the love that God has for us when he wrote, *"but that He has loved us."* In this second phrase, He used the aorist tense in order to denote the timeless nature of this action. God has simply loved us not because of righteous things we have done, but because He is Love. Paul confirms this truth when he writes, *"But God demonstrates His own love for us in that when we were still sinners, Christ died for us"* (Romans 5:8). God's act of sending Christ to die for us is an awesome portrayal of His love.

Often times it is easy to simply focus on the death of Christ and make it supremely significant in understanding God's love. Though the sacrifice God made certainly does grant us great understanding into the love of God, the result of Christ's death grants us great insight also. In the old covenant, sacrifices were provided so that people could be outwardly clean before God (Hebrews 9:13). This outward cleansing enabled God to remain encamped in their midst without having to destroy them because of their sin (including sin done in ignorance…Leviticus 4:1-35) . Nevertheless, it did not allow them to enter into close fellowship with God. God dwelt in their midst within the most holy place inside the tabernacle (which was a supremely holy location inside an extremely holy tent), but they were not allowed to freely enter into this place. A much greater sacrifice was needed in order to enable people to come near to God. This greater sacrifice was accomplished in Christ and was confirmed through the opening of the way into the most holy place when Jesus died and the veil was torn in two (Matthew 27:51, Hebrews 10:17-22). Because of what Jesus did, we are able to have close fellowship with God. John describes this fellowship as 'being alive' when he wrote, *"God sent His only begotten son into the world that we might become alive through Him."* God loved us so much that He didn't merely forgive us of our sins, He made us alive to Himself. He enabled us to know Him personally and have close communion with Him. No one has shown us greater love than to sacrifice everything in order that we might escape wrath and find life in the joy of walking near to God.

Have you known love as John has described it in these passages? Understanding God's love is so pivotal to the Christian life that apart from it a person is dead. God's love is the breath of life which empowers us to live. It is His love that is the nourishing sap from the vine which produces the fruit of good works in our lives. When we come to know God's love, it assures our confidence in Him so that we are able to trust Him despite the most difficult circumstances. This trust eliminates fear and anxiety in our lives and keeps us from believing the lies of the world which will destroy us. Therefore, our level of maturity in Christ will be displayed in how well we have come to know and trust in His love.

Questions to Ponder...

1. Do I think I need to earn God's love? ...why?

2. How does God love me?

Day 28

My dear loved ones, if God so loved us, we also ought to love one another. No one has ever seen God; if we are loving one another, God is abiding in us and His love is matured in us. In this, we know that we are abiding in Him, and He in us, because He has given to us from His spirit. (1 John 4:11-13)

God has made such a variety of different people in this world that it can be hard to relate to them all. Some communicate differently than us. Others have had extremely different life experiences than ours. Still others, simply think differently than we do. Though such differences can be very annoying to us at times, we are still called to walk in love. When we come to see the expressions of God's loving patience and mercy that He has displayed to us, it teaches us how to show the same love toward others. When we are loving others like God has loved us, His presence in our lives becomes a witness to all who have not seen Him.

As John has already written, *"No one has ever seen God."* This includes us. We have not seen the Father in all His heavenly glory, nor has anyone else except Jesus (John 1:18). Nevertheless, though we cannot see the Father through physical eyes, we can still experience Him through His Spirit. Much like eyes or ears or touching something with physical hands, experiencing God in the Spirit is a tangible reality. When God is abiding in us through His Spirit, His love, heart, and will become known. However, just like people's physical senses have to be trained to understand the world around them, so too, we must learn to discern the Spirit of God. Through reading the scriptures and with help from other believers we can learn to spiritually see God while abiding in His Spirit.

When we abide in the Spirit of God it will be evidenced through our love for others. This love does not merely extend to those who are fellow believers, but also to our enemies. For Jesus said, *"If you love the ones loving you, what benefit is that to you? For even sinners love the ones loving them. And if you do good to the ones doing good to you, what benefit is that to you? For even sinners do the same. And if you lend to those from whom you hope to receive, what benefit is that to you? Even sinners lend to sinners, to receive back the same amount. But love your enemies, and do good, and lend not hoping to get repaid, and your reward will be great, and you will be sons of the Most High, because He is kind to the ungrateful and the evil. Be merciful, just as your Father is merciful"* (Luke 6:32-36). The kind of love that we are called to walk in exceeds that of unbelievers. Only the effect of abiding in God can bring us to love as the Father does.

God's love has a transforming effect on our lives and must be matured in us. It is not our love that is matured in us but His love, which is given to us from His spirit. Like the baking of a pie in the oven, once the heat has had its full effect, the pie will give off a pleasing aroma to those who smell it. In the same way, when God's love has had its full effect on us, it changes us, so that we have the fragrance of Christ (2 Corinthians 2:14-16). This fragrance smells like love, joy, peace, patience, kindness, goodness, faithfulness, gentleness, and self control (Galatians 5:22-23). As we continue to grow and are matured by God's love, we will come to bear His image to a world that has not seen Him.

Has the maturing effect of God's love for you been evident in your life? If so, your life will be characterized by love for others. Not simply a love that cares for those who love you in return, but a love that transcends all understanding. If you wrestle with loving others who inconvenience you and make your life difficult, consider how much God has gone out of His way for you, and how much difficulty that you caused Jesus when He died. Remember how much God has loved you and in view of His love, offer yourself as a living sacrifice in love for others. Follow Jesus' instruction and be merciful, as your heavenly Father is merciful (Luke 6:36).

Questions to Ponder...

1. Has God's love had a spiritual maturing effect on my life?

2. Do people come to see God by the way I live among other Christians?

Day 29

And we have seen and testify that the Father has sent the Son, the Savior of the world. Whoever agrees that Jesus is the Son of God, God abides in him, and he in God. (1 John 4:14-15)

A vast number of people in the world agree and openly confess that Jesus is the Son of God. In fact, many seem to think giving lip service to Jesus will make Him come into their heart. Such people who rely upon a confession often don't have lives that evidence God's abiding presence within them. Much in the same way, even demons frequently confess throughout the gospels that Jesus is the Son of God. However, John is certainly not saying that the ungodly and demons have God abiding in them. Therefore, the kind of agreement and confession that John speaks of must be much deeper than simple acknowledgement. Rather it is the kind of agreement that demonstrates full confidence in the reality of Jesus' identity.

James addresses this full confidence when he writes, *"... faith by itself, if it does not have a demonstration in works, is dead. But someone will say, 'You have faith and I have works.' Show me your faith apart from your works, and I will show you my faith by my works. You have confidence that God is one; you do well. Even the demons have this confidence and shudder!"* (James 2:17-19). If the demonstration of our faith is only a verbal agreement, it is demonic. For this is how the demons professed Christ: "And the unclean spirits, whenever they saw him, they fell down before him and cried out saying, 'You are the Son of God' " (Mark 3:11)(see also Luke 4:41 and Matthew 8:29). Demons believe and confess, but walk contrary to the will of God. If we live the same way, we will share in their fate on the day of judgment when we hear, *"Depart from me, you cursed, into the eternal fire prepared for the devil and his angels"* (Matthew 25:41).

Unlike the demonic profession, true believers live their lives in the reality of Jesus' identity. When the Apostle Paul was converted, his proclamation of Jesus being the Son of God was evidence that his heart toward Jesus had changed: *"And immediately he [Paul] proclaimed Jesus in the synagogues, saying, 'He is the Son of God.' And all who heard him were amazed and said, 'Is not this the man who ravaged those who called upon this name in Jerusalem? And has he not come here for this purpose, to lead them bound before the chief priests?' But Saul [Paul] was increasing all the more in power, and was perplexing the Jews living in Damascus proving that Jesus is the Christ"* (Acts 9:20-22). Paul's life was radically transformed when he encountered Jesus and he could not help but to testify to what he had experienced. This is the kind of agreement that John speaks of when he says that God abides in those who agree that Jesus is the son of God.

Are you confessing Jesus is the son of God like Paul or like the demons? Do not be deceived. If your actions don't match your words, you are in danger. In Titus 1:16 we read, *"They confess to know God, but they deny Him by their actions. They are detestable, disobedient, and rejected for any good work."* If your life doesn't demonstrate your confession, God sees you as detestable. Fortunately, you don't have to continue living in a dangerous state with God, for as John has testified: God sent Jesus to be the Savior of the world, which includes us. *"Therefore having a great high priest who has passed through the heavens, Jesus, the Son of God, let us hold fast to our confession. For we do not have a high priest who is unable to sympathize with our weaknesses, but one who has been tempted in every way as we are, yet without sin. Therefore, let us approach the throne of grace with boldness, that we may receive mercy and find grace to help in time of need"* (Hebrews 4:14-16).

Questions to Ponder...

1. Do my actions declare my profession of Christ louder than my words?

2. How do I confess that Jesus is the Son of God? ...like Paul or like demons?

Day 30

And we have known and have trusted the love that God has in us. God is love, and the one abiding in love is abiding in God and God in him. In this, love has been matured with us, in order that we might have confidence in the day of judgment because just as Jesus is now, so also are we in this world. There is no fear in love, but matured love casts out fear because fear has torment and the one who is fearful has not been matured in love. (1 John 4:16-18)

People have formulated all kinds of doctrines about what it means to be in Christ, but when they don't root their understanding in 1 John 4:16-18 they are building on sand. Here we read about the key description of what it is like to dwell in God. In this state, God's love is present within us and is bubbling over so as to immerse our whole being in His affection. No other spot in the Bible gives such a simple description of abiding in God. When we come to understand what it means to abide in God, we can examine our life to know if we are in Him.

As John has described, abiding in God is characterized by dwelling in love. Therefore, he writes, *"In this, we know that we are abiding in Him and He in us, because He has given to us from His Spirit"* (1 John 4:13). In Romans 5:5, we read that the thing which God has given to us from His Spirit is love. This love is not our love for God, nor our love for others, but rather God's love for us: *"this is love: not that we have loved God, but that He has loved us..."* (1 John 4:10). We become confident that we are abiding in God when His love for us has been placed within our hearts by His

Spirit.

God's love for us can be experienced much in the same way that a child can dwell in the affectionate care and protection of a parent. This is how Jesus walked on the earth and how he dwells with the Father in the heavenly realms. He exists in perfect communion, experiencing the Father's love, kindness, gentleness, strength, and faithfulness. This existence with the Father is something that we can experience ourselves while we are in this world. When we continually remain in a state of prayer with a thankful heart, it opens the door for us to become just like Jesus. For a state of prayer prepares us to receive from God and a thankful heart is the union of faith and humility which God rewards with His love (Hebrews 11:6, 1 Peter 5:5). By walking in spiritual alertness and thankfulness, we can abide in the loving presence of God just like Jesus.

When we have come to know the Father's love by dwelling in His presence, it casts out all fear of punishment. Therefore, we can find boldness to approach God's throne, obtain mercy, and discover grace to help in our time of need (Hebrews 4:16). Rather than fearing judgment when drawing near to God, we can boldly expect to find mercy and favor. This means that even if we have sinned, we don't have to continue in it, because God is still willing to transform us if we will humbly approach Him for help. Knowing this kind of love allows us to begin walking with God.

Though we can begin to walk with God when we know His love, it is only when we start trusting His love that our walk becomes steady. The knowledge of God's love is like our right foot and our trust in His love is like our left foot. When we have both feet functioning properly, our walk with God becomes stable (Ephesians 4:13-14). John writes, *"And we have known and have trusted the love that God has in us."* This love for us that God has placed within our hearts, is where we must lay the foundation of our faith. The only unshakable confidence that we can have before God comes through this inner witness of the Spirit. Just as it has been written in Romans 8:15-16, *"For you have not received the spirit of bondage again to fear; but you have received the Spirit of sonship, whereby we cry, Abba, Father. The Spirit itself testifies with our spirit, that we are the children of God."* Our adoption as sons is the ultimate expression of God's love (1 John 3:1). It is on account of our trust placed upon this amazing love, that we are able to find stability in our walk with God.

Can your walk with God be described as dwelling in His love for you? If the answer to this question is no, you are not abiding in God. Perhaps you have made the Christian life a set of principles that you seek to follow; maybe the foundation of your faith is misplaced. Whatever the case, God desires that you would abide in Him. You can enter into God's love by humbling your heart and trusting the things that you have come to know by reading first John. If your walk with God is characterized by dwelling in His love, you are abiding in God. Let God's love become fully matured in you, so that you may be transformed into His image and might find stability in this turbulent world.

Questions to Ponder...

1. Do I have any fear in my life? ...why?

2. How does John describe abiding in God? Am I experiencing this?

3. According to John, should I have confidence on the Day of Judgement?

Day 31

We love because He first loved us. If someone might say, "I love God," and he hates his brother. He is a liar. The one not loving his brother whom he can see, is not able to love God whom he cannot see. And this is the command that we have from Him, the one loving God should also love his brother. (1 John 4:19-21)

Love is not the natural response of humans toward God and other people because love is not self seeking and it always perseveres. What people often call love is really just a selfish pursuit that lasts as long as it brings themselves pleasure. Nevertheless, God is calling us to much more and He has taught us about real love by being a good example. When we come to value God's love toward us, we will love Him in return. This love for God is not merely some feeling we have, but rather a tangible demonstration of what is in our hearts toward God. In this way, love for God is expressed when we do what pleases Him.

The things that please God are the things which He commands us to do. For in 1 John 5:3 we read, *"For this is the love of God that we should keep His commands..."* We are deceiving ourselves if we think that God only wants us to have fluffy feelings toward Him. Rather, He wants our lives to demonstrate a heart fully devoted toward His pleasure. Much like two people who are married, a husband or a wife doesn't want to have a spouse who only has some feelings toward them. Instead, they desire to have a spouse who will lay down their desires and pursuits to prove that they really care for them. In the same way, God wants us to lay down our lives to demonstrate our loving desire to do what pleases Him by obeying His commands.

In 1 John 3:23, we come to understand the summation of God's commands: *"And this is His command that we trust in the name of His son Jesus Christ and we love one another, just as He gave the commandment to us"* (1 John 3:23). Loving God is obedience to His commands and He commands that we walk in love toward others. Therefore, those who truly love God are the ones who will say on the day of judgment, *"... 'Lord, when did we see you hungry and feed you, or thirsty and give you drink? And when did we see you a stranger and welcome you, or naked and clothe you? And when did we see you weak or in prison and visit you?' And the King will answer and say to them, 'Truly, I say to you, as you did it to one of the least of these my brothers, you did it to me'"* (Matthew 25:37-40). Since God Himself is not physically present on earth, He has given us other people through which we can express our love toward Him.

Do you say that you love God? If your life is not a demonstration of love for others, John calls you a liar. No one can love God in a tangible way without loving the real people that He created for us to love. Nevertheless, if you find that love is not in your heart for others, take another glimpse at how much God has loved you. God has not called us to simply love without being loved; rather He has loved us first so that we might have love within us. When we take our eyes off of people and place them onto the God who cares for us, we will find the love we seek for others (Hebrews 12:2-3).

Questions to Ponder...

1. How does my life show that I love God?

2. Do I actually love others because God loves me?

Day 32

Everyone believing that Jesus is the Christ is born of God. Everyone loving the Father, loves those who are born from Him. In this we know that we love the children of God, when we are loving God and doing His commands. For this is the love of God: to keep His commands and His commands are not burdensome. (1 John 5:1-3)

John describes loving people as loving God. These two things are so closely tied together that they are inseparable. When someone loves God, the expression of their love for Him is loving others. Love is an action and if a person has love, it means that their life contains the demonstration of love. When Paul described love in 1 Corinthians 13, he used examples of things that people can do. Some of these examples include showing patience and kindness. In addition, Paul also described love as not doing some actions. Some of these include not envying, not boasting, and not being selfish. When God commands people to love others, he is saying that they must do the things Paul has written about in 1 Corinthians 13. It brings great joy to God when people keep His commands. Therefore, those who desire to please God, will express their love for Him through obedience to His commands.

Much in the same way that the expression of people's lives can show that they love God, it can also show that they don't. Jesus sheds light on how to examine people when he said, *"For no good tree bears rotten fruit, nor does a rotten tree bear good fruit, for each tree is known by its own fruit. For figs are not gathered from thorn bushes, nor are grapes picked from a bramble bush. The good person, out of the good treasure of his heart produces good, and the evil person, out of his evil treasure produces evil, for out of the abundance of the heart his mouth speaks"* (Luke 6:43-45). Jesus is saying that a person's actions are like the fruit that is on a tree. If that person's actions are corrupt and evil, it shows that their heart is full of corruption and evil. If their actions are good and loving, it shows that their heart is full of love and other good things. Therefore, if a person is saying that they have love for God in their heart, it will be evidenced by the display of selfless patience (love) in their life.

John further describes the evidence of having God's love in one's heart as not considering it a bother to do the things that please God. When two people are in love with each other, no one has to tell them to do nice things for each other. They are simply captivated by their partner and as a result don't feel the burden that they carry for each other. Such people will travel across land and sea just to be with each other. No matter what the cost they will see it as worthwhile, just to share their love. In the same way, when a person and God are in love, they will not see it as a burden to sacrifice everything to share in that love. It is for this reason that Jesus was willing to give up His life for those whom He passionately loved.

Do you really love God? If you do, then you will act just like Jesus did. He loved you so much that He sacrificed everything for you. He loved you with a perfect love and He wants you to love Him in the same way in return. If you see it as a burden to please God by doing His commands, then you may fear Him, but you don't love Him. God is desiring to walk in a loving relationship with you and He has already gone the extra mile to show you His love. The question is: will you love Him in return?

Questions to Ponder...

1. Why is it that John ultimately describes loving God and His children as keeping God's commands?

2. Are God's commands a burden to me? ...why?

3. What is the implications of me not loving the children of God or someone I know not loving the children of God?

Day 33

For everyone who has been born of God overcomes the world. This is the victory that overcomes the world, our trusting. Who is it that overcomes the world? Only the one who trusts that Jesus is the son of God.
(1 John 5:4-5)

In this passage, John makes a bold statement that many professing Christians today deny both with actions and their words. This statement is that EVERYONE who has been born of God overcomes the world. So many people live in complete bondage, yet they think that they have been born of God. Such people are deceived. Those who are in bondage to the world are not alive in Christ, but dead in sin. Only through faith and trusting God can people overcome the world.

Faith and trusting are the means by which people lay hold of intimacy with God. Intimacy with God is a form of grace that transforms men and women so that they hate sin and love righteousness. Proverbs explains how intimacy can transform people when it says, *"Whoever walks with the wise becomes wise, but the companion of fools will suffer harm"* (Proverbs 13:20). If we walk with the one who has all wisdom, we become wise like Him. Those who are truly born of God walk with God in ever closer fellowship. As they grow closer to Him, His character and ways rub off on them. Nevertheless, in order to come to this wonderful place with God, people must first trust Him.

Faith or trusting is the key to victory over the world, because when someone trusts God, they stop believing their own thoughts. The mind of man is full of corruption. Even those who have not indulged in gross immoral sins have not escaped the perversion of wrong thinking. This is why it is written, *"Trust in the LORD with all your heart, and do not lean on your own understanding. In all your ways acknowledge him, and he will make straight your paths. Be not wise in your own eyes; fear the LORD, and turn away from evil"* (Proverbs 3:5-7). Here, the instruction is to reject natural self confident human reasoning and instead, trust God and consider His ways when making decisions.

When people stop trusting themselves, it keeps them from being ruled by their own natural desires because they no longer listen to their human desires when making decisions. Those who gain victory over their natural desires have learned the secret to overcoming the world: *"For everything in the world: the desires of the flesh, the desires of the eyes and the proud boasting of what one has and does, comes not from the Father but from the world"* (1 John 2:16). The world consists of desires that don't come from the Father. Therefore, victory over the world can be summed up as overcoming natural desires that don't originate from God. In a practical sense, this means when a man is tempted to look upon a woman to lust after her, he does not do it because he trusts that God knows what is best in saying that he should not (Matthew 5:28). When God says people should not worry about tomorrow, those who trust Him aren't anxious about the future. This applies all across the board in every aspect of life. All forms of sin are linked to corrupted desires and those who overcome the world stop obeying these desires by trusting God.

Have you overcome the world? Are you continuing to overcome the world? If you have not, then you have not been born of God and you need to repent. This is to say that you need to change your thinking. Stop believing your own natural desires and start trusting what God says. It is only when you live your life believing what is written in the Bible, that you will come to have the intimate fellowship with God that will deliver your soul. If you are overcoming the world, don't become lazy in your faith.

"For, yet a little while, and the coming one will come and will not delay; but my righteous one shall be alive by faith, and if he shrinks back, my soul has no pleasure in him." (Hebrews 10:37-38)

Questions to Ponder...

1. Do I overcome the world?

2. According to what John wrote, does my victory over the world indicate that I have been born of God?

3. What is the key to attaining victory over the world?

4. How can I help other lay hold of victory over the world?

Day 34

This is the one that came through water and blood: Jesus Christ, not in the water only, but in the water and in the blood and it is the Spirit that testifies because the Spirit is the truth. There are three that testify: the Spirit, the water, and the blood and these three are in one accord. If we receive the testimony of men, the testimony of God is greater because it is the testimony that God has testified concerning His son. (1 John 5:6-9)

God has not left us without witnesses to the things that have happened with regard to Jesus' first coming. God has done this through both the testimony of men and the testimony of the Holy Spirit. All men are therefore without excuse, because both man's testimony and the testimony of God are in one accord. This united testimony is that Jesus was a man of flesh and blood who came from the Father to bring us life. When we believe this testimony presented to us about Jesus, we will find victory to overcome the world.

Jesus' coming was marked by both water and blood. He was totally human. When Mary groaned in the pains of child birth, Jesus was born just like every other child: in both water and in blood. Though Mary was a virgin, she testified with Joseph that she gave birth to Jesus and he grew up as a man. Hebrews makes it plain why Jesus had to come this way: *"Since therefore the children share in flesh and blood, He likewise shared in the same things, that through death He might render powerless the one who has the control of death, that is, the devil, and deliver those who through fear of death all their life were subject to bondage. ...Wherefore, He was obligated to be made completely like His brothers, so that He might become a merciful and faithful high priest toward God, to satisfy the wrath on account of the sins of the people. For because He has suffered when tempted, He is able to help those who are being tempted"* (Hebrews 2:14-18). Christ's humanity made Him able to satisfy God's wrath on account of our sins. His humanity enabled Him to grant freedom and deliverance from the world and its ruler, the Devil. Apart from Christ's coming as a man we would be lost in our sins.

The testimony that Jesus came as a man was also testified to by John himself when Jesus died on the cross. In John's gospel he wrote, *"...they came to Jesus and as they saw that He was already dead, they did not break His legs. But one of the soldiers pierced His side with a spear, and immediately out came blood and water. The one who has seen this has testified and his testimony is true. He knows that he is telling the truth, in order that you also may believe"* (John 19:33-35). John saw that Jesus not only lived as a man, but that He died as a man as well. In this way, Jesus was the perfect sacrifice for us and His death was real. Unlike the deceivers of John's day who claimed that Jesus didn't come in the flesh, John affirms that Jesus came in full humanity and that we can have confidence on the basis of his testimony.

Nevertheless, John says that if we believe the testimony of man, the testimony of God is greater. This greater testimony has come through the Holy Spirit. The Holy Spirit has borne witness through the miracles that Jesus performed, the fulfillment of prophesy, and His indwelling in the hearts of believers. In all that has been accomplished, the Holy Spirit testifies that Jesus' death has brought reconciliation with God so that we can have fellowship with the Father and His son. This testimony is spoken of in Hebrews 10:15-23, *"The Holy Spirit also testifies to us, for afterward He has said: 'This is the covenant I will make with them after those days, says the Lord. I will place My laws on their hearts, and I will write them on their minds.' and 'Their sins and lawlessness I will remember no longer.' And where there is forgiveness of these, there is no longer a sacrifice for sin. Therefore, brothers, having confidence to enter the Most Holy Place by the blood of Jesus, by a new and living way through the curtain, that is, His flesh, which was dedicated for us and having a great priest over the house of God, let us draw near with a true heart in complete confidence of faith, having our hearts sprinkled to cleanse us from an evil conscience and having our bodies washed with pure water. Let us hold firmly to the hope of our confession, for He who promised is faithful.*" Here we read how we are able to enter into the Most Holy Place (the presence of God) because Jesus had flesh and blood. The Holy Spirit speaks the truth and we can find great assurance of Jesus' humanity because of this testimony.

Do you believe Jesus came as a man? John warns us saying, *"...many deceivers have gone out into the world, not agreeing with Jesus Christ's coming in the flesh. This one is the deceiver and the antichrist. Watch yourselves, so that you may not destroy what we have agonized for, but that you may lay hold of a full reward"* (2 John 1:7-8). There are many who have been deceived into thinking Jesus was not fully human and those who believe this lie will not receive their reward. Jesus was fully man and because of His humanity, He understands our struggles and is able to help us walk righteously: *"For because He has suffered when tempted, He is able to help those who are being tempted"* (Hebrews 2:18). Therefore, let us boldly approach the throne of grace that we might receive the help we need to overcome the world.

Questions to Ponder...

1. Do I believe that Jesus was a man?

2. What is the significance of Jesus coming as a man?

Day 35

*Those who are believing in the Son of God have this
testimony in themselves. The ones not believing God
have made Him out to be a liar, because they have not
believed the testimony which God has testified concerning His Son. This is the testimony: God has given
us eternal life and this life is in His Son. The one who
has the Son has life, the one who does not have the
Son of God does not have life. (1 John 5:10-12)*

No greater assurance can come than the inward testimony
of the Holy Spirit. For no peace truly surpasses all understanding like the one from God Himself. When people experience
the testimony of God in their hearts, they come to know life.
Though many try to find life in their favorite doctrines, a set of
standards, family, and religious holidays, true life is only found in
Jesus Christ Himself.

In John's gospel, he quoted Jesus saying, *"I am the way, the
truth, and the life. No one comes to the Father, except through me"*
(John 14:6). Though people like to believe there are many ways
to God, those who do so call Jesus a liar, because they refuse to
believe what He says about Himself. God has not provided any
other way that people can be reconciled to Himself. The rift of
sin has simply caused people to be so distant from God that no
other religion has anything in it that could bridge the enormous
gulf. Jesus' death and resurrection are the only things that have
the power to reunite humanity into perfect fellowship with the
Holy God of the universe.

Fellowship with God is not some side pursuit for those seeking eternal life. Rather, fellowship with God is eternal life. This can be seen when Jesus said, *"and this is eternal life: that they might know you, the only true God and Jesus Christ whom you sent"* (John 17:3). John further emphasizes this point here in 1 John 5:11 when he writes, *"This is the testimony: that God has given us eternal life and this life is in His Son."* Many have placed the emphasis of eternal life on eternity, but John places the emphasis on life. The Greek word chosen for life in this passage is ζωη (zoe). It refers to the living breathing vitality of a being. When John writes of eternal life, he is speaking of a vitality and consciousness of God. This kind of conscious knowledge of God only comes when we abide in Jesus.

Abiding in Jesus is the experience of eternal life. Therefore, John says, *"the one who has the Son has life, the one who does not have the Son of God does not have life"* (1 John 5:12). Eternal life is so intrinsically tied to Jesus that it doesn't exist apart from Him. When we abide or remain in fellowship with Jesus we have and experience this eternal life. This living fellowship with Jesus is possible only through the Holy Spirit. After Jesus left the earth, He sent the Holy Spirit through whom people can know Jesus and the Father (Ephesians 2:18; John 16:13-15). Nevertheless, Luke quotes Peter in Acts saying that God gives the Holy Spirit to those who obey Him (Acts 5:32). Those who want to know God and have eternal life must humble their will and become trustingly obedient to Him.

Is the Holy Spirit in your heart enabling you to have fellowship with God? If not, you don't yet believe in Jesus. For John says that those who believe in Jesus have this testimony of eternal life within themselves. God desires you to know Him and to experience life forever, but in order to walk with God in fellowship with Him, you must obediently seek to follow Him. Jesus describes true following when he says, *"If any man serves Me, let him follow Me; and where I am, there shall My servant also be..."* (John 12:26). When we follow Jesus, we lose the option to do whatever we want because we must find out where He is and then come to where He is at. Only a diligent pursuit to follow Jesus will be rewarded with the gift of the Holy Spirit to make it possible. Nevertheless, beware, for if you try to lead God around, you will only find that you are nowhere near Him and that you don't have eternal life.

Questions to Ponder...

1. How does John understand eternal life?

2. What other ways or terms does John use in his letter to describe eternal life?

3. How do I know that God's testimony concerning eternal life is in me?

Day 36

I write these things to you who believe in the name of the Son of God that you may perceive that you have eternal life. (1 John 5:13)

Throughout this book, John gives several reasons why he was writing. He wrote to make people's joy complete, to help people turn from sin, and to remind them of the truth. Nevertheless, all the things John has written about can be summed up in this verse. For his overall goal was to make sure that his readers would be able to perceive that they have eternal life.

Eternal life is one of the most confused terms today and likely it was not well understood in John's day either. Many times people see eternal life as going to heaven and not going to hell. They think that eternal life is only something that will come in the future some day. Nevertheless, such people have totally missed all of what John has written about in this letter. John did not write that he wanted people to perceive that they will have eternal life, but that they may perceive that they currently have eternal life. Eternal life is not merely going to heaven in the future, but it is something people can live and experience while they are on the Earth.

John desired to help people know if they are experiencing this life right now and so he gave a few indicators to help people perceive this. The main indicator that He stresses is obedience. John writes, *"In this we know that we have come to know Him, if we keep His commands"* (1 John 2:3). No one can walk in fellowship with God (i.e. have eternal life) without obeying what He says. This is one of John's key methods for showing if someone has eternal life, for he also writes, *"By this it is evident who are the children of God, and who are the children of the devil: everyone who is not doing righteousness is not from God, nor is the one not loving his brother"* (1 John 3:10). John further drives home his point by writing, *"We know that everyone who has been born of God does not keep on sinning, but God keeps the one having been born from Him and the evil one cannot touch him."* (1 John 5:18). People who are in Christ and experiencing life can't say that the devil made them sin because God guards the path His followers are walking on. Overall, if someone has eternal life, it will be indicated by their actions.

A believer's actions are like the fruit which come from a vine. Therefore, Jesus says, *"I am the vine, you are the branches. The one remaining in me and I in him, he will bear much fruit. Apart from me you can do nothing. If anyone does not remain in me, he is like a branch that is thrown away and withers. These branches are gathered up, thrown into the fire, and burned"* (John 15:5-6). The life people have in this age will be the life they have forever. If someone is experiencing life in Christ in this world, they will continue to experience it for eternity. However, if they are not experiencing life in this age, they are like a branch that is withering and will ultimately be burned. They live in spiritual death and for eternity they will experience this death, burning in hell.

John did not want anyone to experience this death and so he has written to you that you may not face eternal judgment, but rather find eternal life. Please examine the fruit of your life and see if you are making every effort to be found in Christ. As you read and study first John and the other books of the Bible, let them be a measuring stick to see if you fit the description of having eternal life. Follow Paul's advice to the Corinthian church when he wrote, *"Test yourselves, to see whether you are in the faith. Prove yourselves. Or do you not fully know this about yourselves, that Jesus Christ is in you?--unless you fail to meet the test!"* (2 Corinthians 13:5).

Questions to Ponder...

1. What did John write to help me perceive if I have eternal life?

2. Does the things that John wrote bring me to confidence that I have eternal life? ...why?

3. How does 2 Peter 1:5-10 instruct me to find assurance?

Day 37

And this is the confidence which we have toward Him, that if we ask anything according to His will, He hears us, and if we perceive that He hears whatever we asked, we perceive that we have the request which we asked from Him. (1 John 5:14-15)

Christianity today is often missing this powerful reality of asking and receiving. Even those who claim to walk in this reality often fall prey to a different gospel than the one of which Jesus spoke. These people believe a gospel of prosperity, thinking that God's intent is to give them all the material riches they ask for. Nevertheless, these people often neglect to seek the true riches from the Holy Spirit. The things from the Holy Spirit are love, joy, peace, patience, kindness, goodness, faithfulness, gentleness, and self control (Galatians 5:22-23). Those who believe the prosperity gospel are often lacking these priceless things from the Holy Spirit. However, Christians should not discredit what John is writing about based solely upon the poor example presented by those who believe this prosperity message.

Though there are many poor examples today, Jesus still remains a perfect example. Jesus was always aware that His Father heard Him and therefore He always received what He asked when it was according to His Father's will. This can be seen when Jesus raised Lazarus from the dead: *"Therefore they took away the stone. And Jesus lifted up His eyes and said, 'Father, I thank you that you have heard Me. I have perceived that You always hear Me, but on account of the crowd standing around, I speak, that they may believe that You sent Me.' And having said these things, He cried out with a loud voice, 'Lazarus, come out here'"* (John 11:41-

43). Jesus always walked in tune with His father and as a result He had supernatural authority.

Jesus did not expect that He would be the only one to walk in supernatural authority. For He said, *"...Have faith in God. Truly, I say to you, whoever says to this mountain, 'Be taken up and thrown into the sea,' and does not doubt in his heart, but trusts that what he says is happening, it will be done for him. Because of this I say to you, as much as you pray and ask, trust that you have received it, and it will be done for you"* (Mark 11:22-24). In another passage Jesus said, *"Truly, truly, I say to you, whoever trusts Me will do the works that I do; and he will do even greater things than these, because I am going to the Father. And whatever you ask in My name, I will do it in order that the Father might be glorified in the Son. If you ask me anything in My name, I will do it"* (John 14:12-14). Though Jesus had great power, He teaches that Christians can walk in that same authority.

The key to walking in this authority is being in tune with God, or in other words, abiding in Him. Jesus explained this in John 15:7 saying, *"If you abide in Me, and my words abide in you, ask whatever you wish, and it will come to pass for you."* Believers must remain in constant fellowship with God and have His words permeating their being. In this way, they will have their minds renewed and learn to ask for things according to the will of God (Romans 12:2). For James explains, *"You ask and do not receive, because you ask wrongly, in order to spend it upon your pleasure seeking"* (James 4:3). God is not interested in empowering us to live selfish lives, but He will empower us to advance His kingdom on earth.

Do you experience this confidence in asking and receiving? If not, start believing what God has said. Don't fall prey to false teaching that says miracles and spiritual authority don't exist any more, *"for the kingdom of God is not a matter of talk but of power"* (1 Corinthians 4:20). We can come to walk in the same power that Jesus had if we only trust Him. Therefore, let us consider what he said and believe: "*... Truly, truly, I say to you, as much as you may ask of the Father in My name, He will give it to you. Until now you have asked for nothing in My name. Ask, and you will receive, that your joy may be full*" (John 16:23-24).

Questions to Ponder...

1. If I ask God to do mighty things, Do I believe that He will do it?

2. Does the Bible teach that God will answer my prayers, if I don't believe that He will give me my requests?

3. If God answers requests that are according to His will, what does Romans 12:2 teach about discerning God's will?

Day 38

If anyone sees his bother sinning a sin not unto death, he should ask, and God will give life to him who is not sinning unto death. There is a kind of sin that is unto death. I am not saying you should ask concerning this. All unrighteousness is sin and there is a type of sin that is not unto death. (1 John 5:16-17)

Sin is a broad word encompassing everything that is not righteous. Therefore, it can include the spectrum of wrong things done in ignorance to willful rebellion against God. In this passage, John is not trying to write about the specific unforgiveable sin of the blaspheme of the Holy Spirit, but rather, he is addressing two general categories of sin. One of these categories consists of sins that will prevent us from having fellowship with God. The other category consists of sins which God will walk in the midst of while He is changing us. Certainly, any sin is able to separate us from a right relationship with God, but there is a type of sin that God requires us to completely turn from before we will be able to experience life in Him at all. Because all sin is not equal, John instructs us to deal with it differently among God's people.

The inequality of sin can be seen in the Old Testament law as God prescribed different consequences for various sins. For example, if someone sinned, doing something in ignorance they were able to kill an animal and present it as a sin offering to satisfy the penalty for their wrong doing (Leviticus 4:27-35). On the other hand, if someone was in willful rebellion against God, the penalty was much more severe. In Deuteronomy 13:6-18, Moses instructs the people of Israel to kill those who stop following God and start serving other gods. Though under the New Covenant with Jesus, believers are no longer supposed to kill idolaters, they are still told to respond to various sins differently.

Paul explains in 1 Corinthians 5:11 that believers are to deal with certain sins quite severely: *"But now I write to you not to associate with anyone who is named a brother that is sexual immoral or greedy, or is an idolater, reviler, drunkard, or swindler; with these do not even eat."* Later on, in chapter six verses nine and ten, Paul expresses that those who do these things will not inherit the kingdom of God. God does not have fellowship with these kinds of sinners because they are in willful rebellion against Him. It is this kind of sin that God will not forgive without a thorough repentance (Hebrews 10:26). Therefore, John instructs us not to pray and ask God that He would walk in fellowship with such sinners (i.e. to give life to such sinners).

This grievous state of sinning unto death does not happen suddenly, but rather through a process described in James 1:14-15: *"but each one is tempted by his own desires, being dragged away and allured. And when desire has conceived it is bringing forth sin and sin, being full grown gives birth to death."* This process begins with the desires in one's heart. When a person refuses to trust God and desires to do his or her own will, the first step toward spiritual death has been taken. The sin spawned from this wrong desire is like a fetus in a womb. It will grow and develop over time until it reaches maturity. When sin has reached its maturity it will display itself in rebellion against God. In this state, sin has given birth to spiritual death. Those who have died spiritually have lost all fellowship with God.

When you see a person sinning who claims to have fellowship with God, stop and evaluate what sin you are observing. Is this person doing something in ignorance and immaturity or are they in rebellion against God? If the person needs to grow up, pray for them and God will give them life. However, if this person is spiritually dead, it may be time to follow God's example and separate yourself from them too. If we deal with sin properly among God's people, we will become most effective in turning sinners from the error of their ways.

Questions to Ponder...

1. Do I see people who claim to be Christians sinning? If yes, how does John teach me to deal with this sin?

2. Am I trying to have Christian fellowship with people who don't have fellowship with God?

3. Is there anyone I should pray for who is growing up in their faith? ...who?

Day 39

We perceive that everyone being born from God is not sinning, but God keeps the one having been born from Him and the evil one cannot touch him. We perceive that we are from God and that the whole world is in the strength of the evil one. (1 John 5:18-19)

Many people have unbiblical ideas about how God defends them from the Devil and therefore they don't understand how John can say that the children of God have victory over sin. These people interpret passages like 1 John 5:18-19 to mean that God will keep them from having evil spirits make them sick and from having their families killed by demons. However, such people have neglected to realize that God did not protect Job from the Devil in these ways (Job 1:12 - 2:10). The protection that John is referring to is from being placed in bondage to sin. Believers are able to overcome sin because God guards the path they walk on and they are not under the power and control of Satan.

Satan has a primary scheme by which he holds the entire world in his strength and control. He rules the world through telling people lies that appeal to their desires (2 Thessalonians 2:9-12). In Ephesians 2:1-3, Paul writes about Satan's ways: *"And you were dead in the trespasses and sins in which you once walked, following the way of this world, following the prince of the power of the air, the spirit that is now at work in the sons of disobedience-- among whom we all once lived in the desires of our flesh, doing the will of the flesh and the mind, and were by nature children of wrath, like the rest of mankind."* Satan is the prince of the power of the air whom the whole world is following. He is leading the world away from fellowship with the Father by encouraging them not to trust God, but to walk according to their own desires. When people live to satisfy their earthly passions, Satan can control them by alluring them through the things of this world.

God protects and keeps His people from Satan's control through wisdom, understanding, and knowledge. Proverbs expresses this truth over and over again: *"...understanding will guard you, delivering you from the way of evil..."* (Provers 2:11-12) and *"Get wisdom; get insight; do not forget, and do not turn away from the words of my mouth. Do not forsake her, and she will keep you; love her, and she will guard you"* (Proverbs 4:5-6) and *"He who trusts in himself is a fool, but he who walks in wisdom is kept safe"* (Proverbs 28:26 NIV). Those who follow God are kept safe by heeding His direction and wisdom.

God has revealed His wisdom through wise men, prophets, angels, the Holy Spirit, and Jesus. Those who desire to have the protection of God in their lives, and to be delivered from the dominion of darkness, must seek after wisdom through these resources. The apostle Paul is one of the prophets whom God has used to bring wisdom to His people. Paul writes, *"My purpose is that they may be encouraged in heart and united in love, unto all the riches of complete understanding, unto a full knowledge of the mystery of God, namely Christ, in whom are hidden all the treasures of wisdom and knowledge. I tell you this so that no one may deceive you by fine-sounding arguments"* (Colossians 2:2-4). Paul brought wisdom by helping people to come to know Jesus Christ. In Jesus, are the wisdom and knowledge that keeps God's people from being deceived and controlled by the Devil.

God has placed His wisdom and knowledge before each of us. Proverbs says, *"Wisdom calls aloud in the street, she raises her voice in the public squares"* (Proverbs 1:20). Nevertheless, will you take the time to listen to wisdom and hide it in your heart? Will you put the full knowledge of God into practice? If not, you have no protection from the Devil and you are rejecting God's method for keeping you safe. Take heed to the words of Paul when he writes, *"Finally, be strengthened by the Lord and in the strength of His might. Put on the whole armor of God, that you may be able to stand against the schemes of the devil. Because we do not wrestle against flesh and blood, but against the rulers, against the authorities, against the cosmic powers of the present darkness, against the spiritual forces of evil in the heavenly places. Therefore, take up the whole armor of God, that you may be able to stand in the evil day, and having accomplished all, to stand firm"* (Ephesians 6:10-13). The armor of God consists of things like truth, the gospel, the word of God, and our confidence in these things. By utilizing these forms of wisdom and knowledge, we will be able to deal with all the flaming arrows of the Devil. Nevertheless, if we reject the protection that God has made available to us, we will not be able to stand and God will let us fall to the dominion of Satan.

Questions to Ponder...

1. What protection have I been relying on?

2. What ways does the Devil attack me?

3. What has God specifically given in order to enable me to stand against my personal battles with the Devil?

$\mathscr{D}ay$ 40

And we perceive that the son of God has come and He has given understanding to us in order that we might know the truth and we are in the truth, in His Son, Jesus Christ. He is the true God and eternal life. Little children, guard yourselves from idols.
(1 John 5:20-21)

The message that John spoke of in the beginning of this letter was that God is light and that there is absolutely no darkness in Him. When people come to have fellowship with God, they escape the darkness and enter into a relationship with truth. God is truth and everything He says and does is true. Unlike the lies and deception that are surrounding everyone living in the world, there is no falsehood in God. Jesus came into the world to be the light that makes truth visible (John 1:1-18).

The Devil is the great deceiver and liar who is seeking to lead the whole world astray. In John 8:44, Jesus called him the father of lies. The darkness these lies create in the world is so thick that apart from Jesus coming and shining light, no one could discern what is true. John describes this when he wrote, *"...we know that the son of God has come and He has given understanding to us in order that we might know the truth"* (1 John 5:20-21). The Greek word in this passage that is translated 'understanding' is most frequently translated 'mind' in the New Testament. The word itself means the faculty of reasoning. Therefore, John is saying that Jesus has brought a new mind through which people can now know truth. Those who have not received this new mind cannot comprehend truth.

Jesus made this new mind available to those who trust Him by giving them the Holy Spirit. Paul explains this when he writes, *"...we have not received the spirit of the world, but the Spirit who is from God, that we might understand the things freely given us by God. We speak these things, not in the words that man's wisdom teaches, but that which the Holy Ghost teaches; interpreting spiritual things with spiritual words. The natural man does not receive the things of the Spirit of God, for they are foolishness to him, and he is not able to know them because they are spiritually discerned"* (1 Corinthians 2:12-14). Apart from the Spirit of God illuminating truth by giving His people a new mind, everyone would be hopelessly deceived by the lies of the Devil.

The Devil is out to trick every person into believing a lie that will draw them away from God. Nevertheless, by continually having fellowship with the truth, people can learn to discern how to remain near to Him who is truth. One of the main ways that the Devil seeks to lead people astray is by hiding God's true nature and character. The Devil does this by creating new gods to replace the one true God: gods that say people don't have to obey the teachings from the Bible; gods who just want everyone to please themselves and be happy. John warns his readers against following such deceit when he writes, *"Little children, guard yourselves from idols"* (1 John 5:21). Throughout this letter, John explains who God is and what He has done. Then in this final phrase, he gives the warning, not to believe a lie.

Have you substituted the truth of God's character for a lie? Jesus' passionate love for you expects that you will love Him the same way in return (1 John 4:11, 5:2). Don't be deceived, He wants all of your heart, all of your mind, and all of your energy (Mark 12:30). Jesus jealously longs that you would walk in fellowship with Him and He gave up His own being to make it possible. After you have come to know the extent of what Jesus has done in pursuing a loving relationship with you, He holds you extremely accountable to respond with the same passionate pursuit toward Him. If you don't respond to the kindness God has shown you in Christ, beware of Paul's warning in Romans 2:4-11: *"...do you despise the riches of his kindness, tolerance, and long suffering, not knowing that the kindness of God leads you unto repentance? But according to your callous and unrepentant heart, you are storing up wrath for yourself in the day of wrath and revelation of the righteous judgment of God. When He gives to each one according to what they do. To those who by endurance in doing good seek glory, honor, and immortality, He will give eternal life. But to those who are self-seeking and un-persuaded by the truth, but are persuaded by unrighteousness, He will give wrath and anger. He will grant torment and distress on every soul of man that does evil, first to the Jew and then to the Greek, but glory, honor, and peace to everyone doing good, first to the Jew and then to the Greek. For God does not show favoritism."* Don't believe the lie about Jesus that says His mercy extends to those who are going their own way. You must come in brokenness, seeking Him with all your heart. Then you will find His mercy and He will give you a new mind that will enable you to intimately know Him (James 4:10).

Questions to Ponder...

1. Based on the things that I have learned from 1 John, have I substituted the real Jesus for things that make me comfortable?

2. How has the real Jesus been challenging me over the last couple weeks to become like Him?

3. How will I be guarding myself against substitutes for Jesus in the future?

Appendix

1 John

1 ¹That which was from the beginning, which we have heard, which we have seen with our eyes, which we have looked at and our hands have touched – concerning the word of life. ²The life appeared and we have seen it and testify to it and we proclaim to you the eternal life which was with the Father and has appeared to us. ³That which we have seen and heard we proclaim to you too, so that you also may have fellowship with us. And our fellowship is with the Father and with His son, Jesus Christ. ⁴We write this to make our joy complete.

⁵This is the message we have heard from Him and proclaim to you: God is light; there is no darkness in Him at all! ⁶If we say we have fellowship with Him yet walk in the darkness, we lie and are not doing the truth. ⁷But if we are walking in the light, as He is in the light, we have fellowship with one another, and the blood of Jesus, His Son, is cleansing us from all sin. ⁸If at any point in time we might say that we don't currently have sin, we are deceiving ourselves and the truth is not in us. ⁹If perhaps we are confessing our sins, He is faithful and just and will forgive us our sins and purify us from all unrighteousness. ¹⁰If at any point, we should say that we have never sinned, we make Him out to be a liar and His word is not in us.

2 ¹My dear children, I am writing these things to you so that you might not sin. But if anybody does perhaps sin, we have an advocate with the Father, Jesus Christ, the Righteous One. ²He is the atoning sacrifice for our sins, and not for ours only but also for the sins of the whole world.

³In this we know that we have come to know Him, if we are keeping His commands. ⁴The one who says, "I know Him," but is not keeping His commands is a liar, and the truth is not in him. ⁵But if anyone obeys His word, God's love has truly been matured in him. This is how we know we are in Him: ⁶Whoever claims to abide in Him ought to walk just as Jesus walked.

⁷Dear loved ones, I am not writing you a new command, but an old command, which you have had from the beginning. This old command is the word that you have heard.

[8]Again, I am writing you a new command; its truth is in Him and you, because the darkness is passing away and the true light is already shining. [9]Anyone who claims to be in the light, and is hating his brother is still in the darkness. [10]Whoever loves his brother abides in the light, and there is no stumbling block within him. [11]But whoever is hating his brother is in the darkness and walks around in the darkness; he does not perceive where he is going, because the darkness has blinded his eyes. [12]I am writing to you, dear children, because your sins have been forgiven on account of His name. [13]I am writing to you, fathers, because you have known Him who is from the beginning. I am writing to you, young men, because you have overcome the evil one. I have written to you, little children, because you have known the Father. [14]I have written to you, fathers, because you have known Him who is from the beginning. I have written to you, young men, because you are strong, and the word of God abides in you, and you have overcome the evil one. [15]Do not love the world or anything in the world. If anyone loves the world, the love of the Father is not in him. [16]Everything in the world: the desires of the flesh, the desires of the eyes and the proud boasting of what one has and does, comes not from the Father, but from the world. [17]The world and its desires are passing away, but the man who is doing the will of God is abiding forever.

[18]Dear children, this is the last hour; and as you have heard that the antichrist is coming, even now many antichrists have come. This is how we know it is the last hour. [19]They went out from our midst, but they were not really from us. For if they were from us, they would have continued with us; but their going showed that not all of them are from us. [20]But you have an anointing from the Holy One, and all of you perceive the truth. [21]I have not written to you because you do not perceive the truth, but because you do and because no lie is from the truth. [22]Who is the liar? It is the one denying that Jesus is the Christ. Such a man is the antichrist, he denies the Father and the Son. [23]Everyone denying the Son does not have the Father;

the one agreeing with the Son has the Father also. [24]See that what you have heard from the beginning abides in you. If what you heard from the beginning abides in you, you also will abide in the Son and in the Father. [25]And this is what He promised us, eternal life.

[26]I have written these things to you about those who are trying to lead you astray. [27]As for you, the anointing you received from Him abides in you, and you do not need anyone to teach you. But as His anointing teaches you about all things and as that anointing is real, and is not a counterfeit, just as it has taught you, abide in Him. [28]And now, dear children, abide in Him, so that when He appears we may be confident and unashamed before Him at His coming. [29]If you perceive that He is righteous, you know that everyone who is doing what is right has been born of Him.

3 [1]See what sort of love the Father has given to us, that we should be called children of God; and that is what we are. The reason why the world does not know us is because it did not know Him. [2]My dear loved ones, now we are the children of God and what we will be has not yet been made known, but we perceive that when He appears, we will be like Him because we will see Him as He is. [3]Everyone who has this hope in him purifies himself even as He is pure.

[4]Everyone who is sinning is also doing lawlessness and sin is lawlessness. [5]You know that He appeared to take away our sins, and in Him there is no sin. [6]The one abiding in Him is not sinning; the one who is sining has neither seen Him nor known Him. [7]children, do not let anyone deceive you. He who is doing what is right is righteous, just as he is righteous. [8]He who is doing what is sinful is of the devil, because the devil has been sinning from the beginning. The reason the Son of God appeared was to destroy the devil's work. [9]Everyone having been born of God will not continue to sin, because God's seed remains in him; he is not able to go on sinning, because he has been born of God. [10]By this it is evident who are the children of God, and who are the children of the devil: everyone who is not doing righteousness is not from God, nor is the one

not loving his brother. [11]This is the message you heard from the beginning: we should love one another, [12]unlike Cain, who belonged to the evil one and murdered his brother. And why did he murder him? Because his own actions were evil and his brother's were righteous. [13]Do not be surprised, my brothers, if the world hates you. [14]We know that we have passed from death to life, because we love our brothers. Anyone who does not love remains in death. [15]Everyone who hates his brother is a murderer, and you know that no murderer has eternal life abiding in him. [16]This is how we know what love is: Jesus Christ laid down His life for us. And we ought to lay down our lives for our brothers. [17]If anyone has material possessions and sees his brother in need, but closes his heart to him, how can the love of God be in him? [18]Dear children, let us not love with words or tongue but with actions and in truth. [19]In this, we know that we belong to the truth, and we persuade our hearts in His presence. [20]Because, if our hearts condemn us, God is greater than our hearts, and He knows everything. [21]Dear loved ones, if our hearts do not condemn us, we have confidence before God [22]and receive from Him whatever we ask, because we keep his commands and do what pleases Him. [23]And this is His command: to trust in the name of His Son, Jesus Christ, and to love one another as He has commanded us. [24]Those who are keeping His commands are abiding in Him, and He in them. And in this we know that He is abiding in us: by the Spirit He gave us.

4 [1]My dear loved ones, do not trust every spirit, but test the spirits to see if they are from God because many false prophets have gone out into the world. [2]This is how we know the spirit that is from God, every spirit that agrees that Jesus Christ has come in the flesh is from God. [3]Every spirit that does not agree with Jesus is not from God, this is the spirit that is from the Antichrist which you heard is coming and is already in the world.

[4]You are from God, dear children, and have overcome them, because greater is the one who is in you than the one

who is in the world. ⁵They are from the world and therefore speak from the world, and the world listens to them. ⁶We are from God, and those who know God listen to us. Those who are not from God do not listen to us, from this we know the spirit of truth and the spirit of deception.

⁷Dear loved ones, let us love one another, for love comes from God. ⁸Everyone who loves has been born of God and knows God. Whoever does not love does not know God, because God is love. ⁹This is how God's love was displayed among us, God sent His only begotten son into the world that we might become alive through Him. ¹⁰In this is love, not that we have loved God, but that He has loved us and sent His son to be the one who satisfied the judgment on account of our sins. ¹¹My dear loved ones, if God so loved us, we also ought to love one another. ¹²No one has ever seen God; if we are loving one another, God is abiding in us and His love is matured in us.

¹³In this, we know that we are abiding in Him, and He in us, because He has given to us from His spirit. ¹⁴And we have seen and testify that the Father has sent the son, the savior of the world. ¹⁵Whoever agrees that Jesus is the son of God, God abides in him, and he in God. ¹⁶And we have known and have trusted the love that God has in us.

God is love, and the one abiding in love is abiding in God and God in him. ¹⁷In this, love has been matured with us, in order that might have confidence in the day of judgment because just as Jesus is now, so also are we in this world. ¹⁸There is no fear in love, but matured love casts out fear because fear has torment and the one who is fearful has not been matured in love. ¹⁹We love because He first loved us. ²⁰If someone might say, "I love God," and he hates his brother. He is a liar. The one not loving his brother whom he can see, is not able to love God whom he cannot see. ²¹And this is the command that we have from Him, the one loving God should also love his brother.

5 ¹Everyone believing that Jesus is the Christ is born of God. Everyone loving the Father, loves those who are born from Him. [2]In this we know that we love the children of God, when we are loving God and doing His commands. [3]For this is the love of God: to keep His commands and His commands are not burdensome. [4]For everyone who has been born of God overcomes the world. This is the victory that overcomes the world, our trusting. [5]Who is it that overcomes the world? Only the one who trusts that Jesus is the son of God.

[6]This is the one that came through water and blood: Jesus Christ, not in the water only, but in the water and in the blood and it is the Spirit that testifies because the Spirit is the truth. [7]There are three that testify: [8]the Spirit, the water, and the blood and these three are in one accord. [9]If we receive the testimony of men, the testimony of God is greater because it is the testimony that God has testified concerning His son. [10]Those who are believing in the son of God have this testimony in themselves. The ones not believing God have made Him out to be a liar, because they have not believed the testimony which God has testified concerning

His son. [11]This is the testimony: God has given us eternal life and this life is in His son. [12]The one who has the son has life, the one who does not have the son of God does not have life. [13]I write these things to you who believe in the name of the Son of God that you may perceive that you have eternal life.

[14]And this is the confidence which we have toward Him, that if we ask anything according to His will, He hears us, [15]and if we perceive that He hears whatever we asked, we perceive that we have the request which we asked from Him. [16]If anyone sees his bother sinning a sin not unto death, he should ask, and God will give life to him who is not sinning unto death. There is a kind of sin that is unto death. I am not saying you should ask concerning this. [17]All unrighteousness is sin and there is a type of sin that is not unto death.

[18]We perceive that everyone being born from God is not sinning, but God keeps the one having been born from Him and the evil one cannot touch him. [19]We perceive that we are from God and that the

whole world is in the strength of the evil one. [20]And we perceive that the son of God has come and He has given understanding to us in order that we might know the truth and we are in the truth, in His son, Jesus Christ. He is the true God and eternal life. [21]Little children, guard yourselves from idols.

Author's Translation

You may freely use this translation in derivative works as long as you offer it to others free of charge. If you need to cite a reference for a quote simply use this book's title.

WWW.GODLYCHRISTIANMINISTRIES.COM

Free Christian Music
Free Christian e-Cards
More Christian Stuff...

HAVE YOU BEEN BLESSED BY THIS BOOK?
LEARN MORE ABOUT THE AUTHOR
AND FIND MORE RESOURCES HE OFFERS.

Godly Christian Ministries provides a number of
Christian resources to encourage you and spur you on to
know Jesus. Here you will find music, articles, books,
e-cards, audio testimonies, and much more...